Daily Ve

Jewels from The World Peace Diet

Dr. Will Tuttle

Original Art by Madeleine Tuttle

Daily VegInspirations:
Jewels from The World Peace Diet

© 2018 Will Tuttle, Ph.D.
Karuna Music & Arts
1083 Vine Street
Healdsburg, CA 95448

Published by: Karuna Music & Arts; www.willtuttle.com

Cover painting and interior brush paintings: Madeleine Tuttle
All art copyright © 2018 Madeleine Tuttle

Printed in the United States of America

ISBN: 978-0-57842940-3

Daily VegInspirations
Jewels from The World Peace Diet

Dr. Will & Madeleine Tuttle

Dedicated to our fellow mortals,
With appreciation, apologies, and love.

Table of Contents

Foreword

by James Aspey

The World Peace Diet by Dr. Will Tuttle was the first book I read on the topic of veganism and animal rights. The way it was described in an online comment thread is what inspired me to read it: "The most comprehensive book on veganism ever written. Basically, it's the Vegan Bible."

Being new to the topic and instantly passionate and intrigued, I started reading and was deeply moved by the content as well as the way it was written. It covered every step, from breeding animals into existence through rape, to the violent murders that ended their lives of misery inside slaughterhouses. It helped me awaken to the relentless circle of enslavement and exploitation that animals are forced to endure and have been every single day, since long before I was born.

The health dangers of consuming meat, dairy and eggs, as well as the many health benefits of a plant-based diet, were thoroughly explained, as was the highly destructive environmental impact caused by animal agriculture. There are countless benefits our society, environment and culture would stand to gain from healing our severed connection to the earthlings with whom we share this planet.

More than this, the book had a strong spiritual connotation. What I mean when I say it was spiritual is that it's aligned with our spirit, or in other words, the message was aligned with the core of who we are. At our core we are compassionate, loving and kind.

Many of us have lost our way. To make matters worse, powerful corporations are profiting from the separation of our true spiritual nature. They add fuel to the fire by sharing marketing propaganda. They tell us we need meat for protein and dairy for calcium, that fish don't feel pain, that animals are inferior, that animals are killed "humanely," and many other outright lies. No wonder so many people are confused!

We have an enormous job to do.

First, to heal ourselves and our connection to animals by understanding fully the consequences of our choices.

Next, to align our actions with our values and make the shift from foods and products of oppression and violence, to foods and products of peace and kindness.

And finally, to educate, encourage and support others in repairing their severed connection. That's the purpose of this book. Please share the messages within this book with everyone.

Trillions of aware, feeling, intelligent beings are counting on us. If we all do our part, we can finally bring an end to the largest genocide the world has ever known.

September 2018

Introduction
The Golden Key and 366 Jewels

Every day is a gift. In our first waking moment we can plant a seed of inspiration for the adventure that beckons. Our heart warms as we greet the day, giving thanks for another opportunity to learn, and to discover new ways to contribute our unique abilities to the healing and awakening of our world.

This is a book of daily inspirations that are drawn primarily from my book, *The World Peace Diet*. There are also some that came from some of my essays written around the time *The World Peace Diet* was originally published. Each daily reading expresses an understanding that we can contemplate and strive to embody and share as we go through our day. I recommend reading them in the morning as seed-inspirations for the upcoming day, and of course you are free to use them in whatever way feels best for you.

These 366 nuggets of vegan insight and information are well-polished jewels distilling deeper truths that our consciousness can unfold, unpack, and digest through reflection, contemplation, and germination. They can feed us a most nourishing meal, nutriment that comes from within and that manifests as mindful awareness, as compassion, and as inspiration to follow our hearts rather than the well-worn paths of conformity.

The World Peace Diet is intended to be a guidebook into deep veganism, and into the profoundly liberating potential of positive cultural and personal transformation that is hidden within veganism. This word is a contemporary iteration of the ancient wisdom teaching of *ahimsa,* nonharmfulness, and this teaching of nonviolence—widely misunderstood in our world today—is the golden key that opens doorways into freedom, healing, and harmony in our personal and collective lives.

We are living in pivotal and perilous times. *The World Peace Diet* movement aims to provide the deeper understanding we yearn for, creating the foundational context to empower us to build a more conscious world where peace, freedom, justice, sustainability, and radiant health are possible. It is a sword to cut through distressing delusions, and a lantern to illuminate the central hidden fury churning invisibly at the core of our society and destroying not only the beauty and resilience of our Earth, our culture, and our physical health, but also eroding and suppressing our intelligence, sensitivity, creativity, and spirituality. This central and defining destructive force is animal agriculture, and the banquet of consequences upon which we are all dining is the result of not only the practice of abusing and killing millions of animals daily, but also of the mentality required to do this relentlessly, which is injected into all of us from infancy.

Though we have all been wounded by the hidden attitudes and practices required by animal agriculture, we can all help each other to heal through our own individual healing process. At its core, veganism is not any "ism." It is simply doing our best to be a force of kindness and respect, and to bring healing to our bodies, minds, relationships, society, and our Earth.

These vegan inspirations, the Daily VegInspiration, carry the essence of the liberating and transformational message of *The World Peace Diet*. In this book, they are adorned with ink brush paintings by my spouse Madeleine. Madeleine studied the Zen art of *Sumiye* in Japan, and an essential dimension of *Sumiye* Zen brush painting is meditation. Through meditation, the mind becomes quiet, and the brush can capture and reveal the hidden essence of the bamboo, the bird, the flower, the cow.

In addition to the 366 Daily VegInspirations, we are also offering the Seven-Fold Path of World Peace, which follows this introduction. Corresponding to the days of the week., these affirmations can be helpful either separately or in conjunction with the Daily VegInspirations. Engaging with these seven affirmations for several weeks can bring a deeper understanding of the dimensions of vegan living.

We invite you to join us in this adventure of discovery. Through the seed ideas excerpted from *The World Peace Diet* and through the images revealed through the Zen brush, may our minds and hearts be awakened and healed, and may we bring this to our world. Enjoy!

Dr. Will Tuttle, 2018

Seven-Fold Path of World Peace

These seven affirmations for world peace are based on the Eightfold Path, and can be applied each day by contemplating the particular day's affirmation and keeping it in awareness throughout the day.

Monday: the Day of Right Understanding
Questioning our conditioned thinking, we strive to realize the highest understanding that brings liberation and kindness to all living beings.

Tuesday: the Day of Right Aspiration
We aim to realize every situation today as an opportunity to awaken from habitual thinking and to more skillfully benefit others.

Wednesday: the Day of Right Speech
Our inner and outer speech is guided by appreciation for the unity and uniqueness of all expressions of life.

Thursday: the Day of Right Action
We treat others with respect and behave so that we are never uncertain about the kindness and rightness of our actions.

Friday: the Day of Right Livelihood
Our livelihood flows from our highest understanding and aspiration, bringing healing and awakening to our world.

Saturday: the Day of Right Effort
Whatever is appropriate, we persistently make our best effort, and live in harmony with the source of all energy and activity.

Sunday: the Day of Right Mindfulness and Concentration
We function in tranquil one-pointed awareness, cultivating mindful speech and action, and looking and listening with compassion.

Mindfulness Meditation

The Daily VegInspirations

January 1

As we look more deeply at our food, the healing of our children can begin, and our work can be resurrected as an instrument for blessing and bringing joy and caring to our world.

January 2

As we remove the violence from our daily meals, we will naturally increase our ability to heal our divisions, nurture our creativity and joy, restore beauty and gentleness, and be role models of sensitivity and compassion for our children.

January 3

The lesson is plain: when we harden ourselves to the suffering we inflict on animals in our own interest, and justify it by proclaiming our superiority or specialness, it is but a short and unavoidable step to justifying and inflicting the same kind of suffering on other humans in our own interest while likewise proclaiming our supremacy or specialness.

January 4
We are conditioned mentally to disconnect our food from the animal who was mindlessly abused to provide it, but the vibrational fields created by our food choices impact us profoundly whether we pretend to ignore them or not. Practicing mindful eating illuminates these hidden connections, cleanses our mind, heart, and actions, and removes inner masks and armor so that it becomes quite plain to see.

January 5
As the mentality of domination and exclusivism fades, we will be able to heal divisions of gender, race, and class.

January 6
The unremitting conflict and oppression of history are unavoidable byproducts of confining and killing animals for food, as is the male role model of macho toughness that is required of both the professional animal killer (herder) and the soldier. If we desire to eat animal foods, this suffering is the unavoidable price we must pay.

January 7
It's easier to see the gallons of fossil fuel poured directly into our cars than it is to see the gallons of fossil fuel poured into our cheese, eggs, fish sticks, hot dogs, and steaks.

January 8

If we believe absurdities, we will commit atrocities, and we pass it on to our children, generation upon generation. Our violent actions speak so much more loudly than our peaceful words, and this is the unyielding dilemma of the herding culture we call home. The only way to solve this dilemma is to evolve cognitively and ethically to a higher level where our actions do not belie our words and force us into unconsciousness and denial, but rather align with and reinforce our words and the universal spiritual teachings that instruct us to love one another, and to have mercy on the weak and vulnerable rather than exploiting and dominating them.

January 9

To stop the atrocities, we must awaken from the absurd belief that animals are insentient, trivial, soulless property objects and challenge our religious institutions to extend ethical protection to animals. This of course will mean challenging the meals at the center of social and religious life and the atrocities "hidden in plain sight" within those meals.

January 10

Jesus questioned the foundation of war and oppression, which was then, as it is now, the killing and eating of animals. Back then it was animal sacrifice performed by priests at the temple, which was the main source of wealth and prestige for the Jewish religious power structure, as well as being the source of meat for the populace. Jesus' confrontation at the temple in which he drove out those selling animals for slaughter was a bold attack on the fundamental herding paradigm of viewing animals merely as property, sacrifice objects, and food.

January 11

Perhaps in the past people thought they needed to enslave animals and people to survive, and that the cruelty involved in it was somehow allowed them. It's obviously not necessary for us today, as we can plainly see by walking into any grocery store, and the sooner we can awaken from the thrall of the obsolete mythos that we are predatory by nature, the sooner we'll be able to evolve spiritually and discover and fulfill our purpose on this earth.

January 12

A positive approach is essential because it mobilizes our spiritual resources, generates enthusiasm, and brings more joy and love into our world.

January 13

Our knowledge and understanding of nonhuman animals is polluted far more than we acknowledge by our belief in our own superiority, our unrecognized cultural programming, and our separation from nature. Our theories about animals will be seen in the future as quaint balderdash, as we now view the medieval theories of healing through bleeding and leeches and of an earth-centered solar system.

January 14

Grain that is now fed to the livestock of the world's wealthy could feed the starving poor.

January 15

Only by going beyond "it's no big deal" and "it's just a problem like our other problems" will we be able to step outside our conditioning and see the full import of our relentless abuse of animals, recognizing it as the motivating, hidden fury behind our global crisis.

January 16

We must shake the old stagnation and comfortable disconnections out of our minds and bodies, embrace the evolutionary urge within us to awaken compassion and intuitive wisdom, and live our lives in accord with the truth that we are connected intimately with all living beings.

January 17

Love brings freedom, joy, power, grace, peace, and the blessed fulfillment of selfless service. Our true nature, our future self, beckons irresistibly as an inner calling to awaken our capacity for love, which is understanding.

January 18

With love and understanding awakening in us, compassion expands to include ever-larger circles of beings. Compassion may be seen as the highest form of love, for it is the love of the divine whole for all its parts and is reflected in the love of the parts for each other. It includes the urge to act to relieve the suffering of apparent others, and this urge requires us to evolve greater wisdom and inner freedom to relieve suffering more effectively. Compassion is thus both the fruit of evolution and the driving force behind it. Love yearns for greater love.

January 19

Every day, we cause over thirty million birds and mammals and forty-five million fish to be fatally attacked so we can eat them, and it's universally considered to be good food for good people. With these meals, we feed our shadow, which grows strong and bold as it gorges itself on our repressed grief, guilt, and revulsion.

January 20

Liberating and honoring the feminine principle is perhaps the most pressing task in our culture's evolution toward peace, sustainability, and spiritual maturity.

January 21

Living a consequent vegan life naturally encourages us to awaken from the consensus trance that brings unquestioning conformity and allows cruelty and slavery to continue. Refusing to see animals as commodities, we are able to see through countless other pretenses. And, as transformative as this is for an individual to experience, it would be infinitely more transformative for our culture to do so, and to evolve beyond the obsolete orientation that sees animals as mere food commodities.

January 22

Judging by the generally small numbers who have actually gone vegan in our culture, it appears that this commitment requires a certain breakthrough that has been generally elusive because of the mentality of domination and exclusion we've all been steeped in since birth. There is something about veganism that is not easy, but the difficulty is not inherent in veganism, but in our culture.

January 23

Learning to look the other way brings spiritual death in everyone who practices it. In encouraging it, religious institutions show how far they have strayed from the passionate mercy and all-seeing kindness taught and lived by those whose spiritual evolution and illumination inspired the institutions themselves.

January 24

Spiritual teachings of our interconnectedness and the vegan ethic of universal compassion, besides being vital and transformative, are in profound alignment with the core instruction of the world's religions, which is to love others.

January 25

Disconnecting and desensitizing in comfort is not the same as inner peace, which is the fruit of awareness and of living in alignment with the understanding that comes from this awareness.

January 26

Our minds and consciousness are almost completely unexplored territory because we have been raised in a herding culture that is fundamentally uncomfortable with introspection. Our science blatantly ignores consciousness as an unapproachable, unquantifiable and unopenable "black box" and distracts us with focusing solely on measurable phenomena. Our religions discourage meditation and reduce prayer to a dualistic caricature of asking and beseeching an outside, enigmatic, and projected male entity.

January 27

Post-rational intuitive knowing can be born as a sense of being connected with all beings. No longer being merely a parade of conditioned thoughts revolving around a sense of being a separate self, we can sense more deeply into the nature of being and begin to know outside the limitations of linear thinking. With this comes an understanding that our essential nature is not evil, confined, selfish, or petty, but is eternal, free, pure, and is of the essence of love.

January 28

We may discover that we can "think" with our hearts, without words, and we may learn to appreciate the consciousness of animals and begin to humbly explore their mysteries. There is perhaps much we can learn from animals. Not only do they have many powers completely unexplainable by contemporary science, but they are fellow pilgrims with us on this earth who contribute their presence to our lives and enrich our living world in countless essential ways. In fact, without the humble earthworms, bees, and ants whom we relentlessly kill and dominate, the living ecosystems of our earth would break down and collapse—something we certainly cannot say about ourselves!

January 29

As long as we remain imprisoned in the maze of self-oriented thinking, we can easily justify our cruelty to others, excuse our hard eyes and supremacist position, discount the suffering we impose on others, and continue on, rationalizing our actions and blocking awareness of the reality of our feelings and of our fundamental oneness with other beings.

January 30

Eating animal foods is an indefensible holdover from another era beyond which we must evolve, and with the ever-increasing profusion of vegan and vegetarian cookbooks and vegan foods like soy milk, soy ice cream, rice syrup, tofu, veggie burgers, and so forth, as well as fresh organically grown vegetables, legumes, fruits, grains, nuts, pastas, and cereals, we see alternatives proliferating. Books, videos, websites, vegetarian/vegan restaurants and menu options, animal rights groups, and vegan organizations are also multiplying as we respond to the vegan imperative.

January 31

As we all know in our bones, there is a predatory quality to our economic system, and competition underlies all our institutions. We prey upon each other. It may not be obvious from within our planet's dominant society, but our culture and our corporations and other institutions act in ways that can only be described as predatory vis-à-vis those who are less industrialized, less wealthy, and less able to protect themselves.

February 1

Intuition opens the door to healing. It never sees any living being as an object to be used but sees all beings as unique and complete expressions of an infinite universal presence, to be honored, respected, learned from, and celebrated. Intuition is Sophia, the beloved wisdom we yearn for and seek.

February 2

As we prey upon and "harvest" animals, we use and prey upon people, employing euphemisms according to the situation as "foreign aid," "privatization," "advertising," "spreading the gospel," "capitalism," "education," "free trade," "lending," "fighting terrorism," "development," and countless other agreeable expressions. The tender loving heart of our true nonpredatory nature is troubled by all this, but it shines unceasingly, and though it's perhaps covered over by our conditioning, it nevertheless inspires the selfless giving, compassion, and enlightenment that our spiritual traditions expound.

February 3

Our bodies reflect our consciousness, which yearns to unfold higher dimensions of creativity, compassion, joy, and awareness, and longs to serve the larger wholes—our culture, our earth, and the benevolent source of all life—by blessing and helping others and by sharing, caring, and celebrating. We have, appropriately, a physiology of peace.

February 4

We can realize that we are meant to live in harmony with the other animals of this earth because we've been given bodies that actually function better *without* killing and stealing from them. What a liberating gift! No animal need ever fear us, because there is no nutrient that we need that we cannot get from non-animal sources.

February 5

By recognizing and understanding the violence inherent in our culture's meal rituals and consciously adopting a plant-based diet, becoming a voice for those who have no voice, we can attain greater compassion and happiness and live more fully the truth of our interconnectedness with all life. In this we fulfill the universal teachings that promote intelligence, harmony, and spiritual awakening.

February 6

We may become irate that someone would even suggest that our mother's loving meals and our father's barbecues were a form of indoctrination. Our mother and father didn't *intend* to indoctrinate us, just as their parents didn't intend to indoctrinate them. Nevertheless, our old herding culture, primarily through the family and secondarily through religious, educational, economic, and governmental institutions, enforces the indoctrination process in order to replicate itself in each generation and continue on.

February 7

We all know in our bones that other animals feel and suffer as we do. If we use them as things, we will inevitably use other humans as things. This is an impersonal universal principle, and ignoring it doesn't make it go away. It operates with mathematical regularity as Pythagoras taught: what we sow in our treatment of animals, we eventually reap in our lives. Because it is a taboo to say this or make this fundamental connection in our herding culture, we can go to church assured that we will not be confronted by the discomforting entreaty to love all living beings and to use none of them as things.

February 8

To some, simply becoming vegan looks like a superficial step—can something so simple really change us? Yes! Given the power of childhood programming and of our culture's inertia and insensitivity to violence against animals, authentically becoming a committed vegan can only be the result of a genuine spiritual breakthrough. This breakthrough is the fruit of ripening and effort; however, it is not the end but the beginning of further spiritual and moral development.

February 9

From this new consciousness we can accomplish virtually anything; it represents the fundamental positive personal and cultural transformation that we yearn for, and it requires that we change something basic: our eating habits.

February 10

Our life can become a field of freedom and peace as we deepen our understanding of the sacredness and interdependence of all living beings, and practice non-cooperation with those forces that see creatures as mere commodities.

February 11

Looking undistractedly into the animal-derived foods produced by modern methods, we inescapably find misery, cruelty, and exploitation. We therefore avoid looking deeply at our food if it is of animal origin, and this practice of avoidance and denial, applied to eating, our most basic activity and vital ritual, carries over automatically into our entire public and private life. We know, deep down, that we cannot look deeply anywhere, for if we do, we will have to look deeply into the enormous suffering our food choices directly cause.

February 12

Veganism is still exceedingly rare even among people who consider themselves spiritual aspirants because the forces of early social conditioning are so difficult to transform. We are called to this, nevertheless; otherwise our culture will accomplish nothing but further devastation and eventual suicide.

February 13

What is compassion? It is not simply a sense of caring and kindness toward the being before you. It isn't merely a warm-hearted feeling of empathy for the suffering of others. It is also the determined and practical resolve to do whatever is possible to relieve their suffering, the sustained urge to reduce and eliminate the suffering they are experiencing.

February 14

All cultures naturally propagate themselves through their various institutions, and ours is no different. Our scientific, religious, governmental, educational, and economic institutions all reflect the same underlying mentality and reinforce it, which is why veganism is so strenuously resisted, and also why it is so urgently needed as well.

February 15

If our only motivation for not eating animal foods is our own health, it's easy to "cheat" a little here and there and pretty soon go back to eating them again. When our motivation is based on compassion, it is deep and lasting, because we understand that our actions have direct consequences on others who are vulnerable.

February 16

Looking deeply, we see that the perpetrators are themselves victims of violence—that's why they've become perpetrators—and their violence hurts not only the animals but themselves and the bystanders as well. All three are locked in a painful embrace, and it is the bystanders who have the real power. They can either turn and look away, thus giving their tacit approval, or they can witness and bring a third dimension of consciousness and awareness to the cycle of violence that has the victims and perpetrators hopelessly enmeshed.

February 17

Our greatest joy comes in helping others and blessing them, and we hurt ourselves the most when we harm others for our own gain.

February 18

With awareness, our behavior naturally changes, and individual changes in behavior, rippling through the web of relationships, can lead to social transformation and bring new dimensions of freedom, joy, and creativity to everyone. It all begins with our most intimate and far-reaching connection with the natural order, our most primary spiritual symbol, and our most fundamental social ritual: eating.

February 19

As our hearts open to deeper understanding, our circle of compassion thus automatically enlarges, and spontaneously begins to include more and more 'others.' Not just our own tribe, sect, nation, or race, but all human beings, and not just humans, but other mammals, and birds, fish, forests, and the whole beautifully-interwoven tapestry of living, pulsing creation. All of Us.

February 20

The pollution of our shared consciousness-field by the dark agonies endured by billions of animals killed for food is an unrecognized fact that impedes our social progress and contributes gigantically to human violence and the warfare that is constantly erupting around the world.

February 21

Our cultural predicament—the array of seemingly intractable problems that beset us, such as chronic war, terrorism, genocide, starvation, the proliferation of disease, environmental degradation, species extinction, animal abuse, consumerism, drug addiction, alienation, stress, racism, oppression of women, child abuse, corporate exploitation, materialism, poverty, injustice, and social malaise—is rooted in an essential cause that is so obvious that it has managed to remain almost completely overlooked.

February 22

Question everything this culture says, throw off the chains of harming and stealing from fish, birds, and other mammals, and join the vegan celebration!

We will love this world and each other so deeply that we will all be transformed.

February 23

Our meals and institutions reflect each other and reinforce the delusion that we are violent and competitive by nature. Spiritual and religious teachings say otherwise. The Bodhisattva ideal that Buddhists emulate, for example, embodies the understanding that our true nature is wisdom, loving-kindness and cooperativeness.

February 24

Veganism is the essence of inclusiveness and nonviolence: seeing sacred beings when we see others, never reducing them to objects or commodities for our use. It is the ancient wisdom of the interconnectedness of the welfare of all, and is also the dawning mentality that is foundational to sustainability, freedom, and lasting peace. Our children's world will be vegan, or the alternative is unpleasant to contemplate.

February 25

If lab-grown "meat" becomes available, that will reduce our killing and waste of resources. And it may help us move toward veganism, since our meals will no longer require us to disconnect from the suffering we're causing animals. However, there are countless ways we oppress and abuse animals besides eating them, and if our culture doesn't evolve to the vegan ethic of compassion to all beings, and continues to use and prey on animals, our technology will magnify our violence and we'll do the same to each other.

February 26

When we realize that we've all been given the gift of bodies that require no nutrients we cannot get from plant sources, we can become, ourselves, the change we want to see in the world. This is the heart and soul of the vegan revolution of love, joy, and peace that is beckoning and to which we are all called to contribute.

February 27

There is no greater act of love and freedom than to question the core of violence and disconnectedness churning unrecognized in the belly of our culture, and to switch to a plant-based diet because of compassion for the countless animals, humans, and future generations to whom we are related. All life is interconnected, and as we bless others, we are blessed. As we allow others to be free and healthy, we become free and healthy.

February 28

Each and every one of us makes our world.

February 29

The boundless joy that accompanies leaving the prison of delusion draws us irresistibly, and this joy is ultimately inevitable for everyone. Veganism is love for all, expressed as respect and kindness, and is both the path and the goal of spiritual life. It leads, when practiced mindfully, to the awakening that there is no fundamentally separate self at all. We are all infinitely interconnected manifestations of boundless, radiant love, and we are here to discover and share our unique gifts, and allow this love to shine and flow through us, as the lives we live.

March 1

The destructive agricultural system now in place devastates millions of acres of forest and grassland in order to grow corn, soybeans, wheat, and other grains and legumes for animals, who convert plant carbohydrate into profitable and unhealthy fat and protein. The food and medical industries are guaranteed lucrative incomes at the expense of starving people, wildlife, aquifers, biosystems, and future generations. Ironically, we're growing far more grain than we could ever eat ourselves. The billions of dollars invested in hospitals, drugs, and pharmaceutical and medical facilities require a reliable and steady flow of clogged arteries and cancers to stay profitable and pay back the bankers in the background.

March 2

The destructive agricultural system now in place the self-centered pursuit of pleasure have been behind all the atrocities we humans have committed, and when we shine the light of our awareness and truth on them, they are seen for the weak, erroneous delusions that they truly are.

March 3

The great philosopher Schopenhauer, in criticizing how some Christians treat animals, wrote, "Shame on such a morality that fails to recognize the eternal essence that exists in every living thing, and shines forth with inscrutable significance from all eyes that see the sun." All of us are celebrations of infinite mysterious Spirit, deserving of honor and respect.

March 4

It seems there are three main reasons why people continue to eat animals in spite of the horror and tragedy this behavior generates. The first and essential reason is that eating animals is not a behavior people have ever chosen freely. It has, instead, been forced upon them, starting at an early age. People have been *indoctrinated* to do it. The second reason is because of social pressure. Being so gregarious, we humans like to fit in and be part of the group, and this militates strongly against questioning the eating of animal foods. The third big reason is that people like the taste: they get a certain pleasure that they are loath to give up. Fortunately, these three fundamental reasons for eating animal foods are all ultimately invalid and indefensible.

March 5

In the Japanese language there is a beautiful word, "shojin," roughly translated into English as "abstention from animals foods and products for religious or spiritual reasons." The existence of this word reveals the culture's recognition that abstaining from the use of animal products is a valid dimension of religious practice and of spiritual aspiration.

March 6

Anthropologists refer to the five prohibitions as the five universal taboos, which cross-culturally prohibit, against other humans, the actions of killing, stealing, lying, sexual misconduct, and forcing drugs or toxic substances on others. In our culture today, we are evolving toward an understanding of these prohibitions that includes animals as well: seeing that just as it is a violation to harmfully interfere with Spirit's experience of being a human, it is also a violation to harmfully interfere with Spirit's experience of being an animal.

March 7

As we evolve spiritually, we become more awake to the truth of interbeing, that all living beings are profoundly interconnected, and that by harming others, I harm myself because the life in that apparent 'other' is the same life that lives in this apparent 'me.'

March 8

When love is born in our hearts, we want only the best for others, for we directly see them as ourselves. The imprisoning illusion of a fundamentally separate self, struggling against other selves for its own rewards, is transcended, and our life becomes dedicated to bringing peace, joy, and fulfillment to others. This brings us our greatest joy, and is the flowering of the highest form of love, which is compassion. We must, if this process is actually happening in us, be drawn toward veganism, and it is in no way a limitation on us, but the harmonious fulfillment of our own inner seeing.

March 9

Veganism is not "veganism." That's all looking from the outside. We live, serve, and give thanks for this precious life arising through All of Us. It may look like and be called veganism, but it is not an option. It is simply the expression of our own true nature: seeing beings to be respected rather than things to be used.

March 10

I hope that all vegans or aspiring vegans have the opportunity at some point in our lives to live in a vegan community for a while. I have had this opportunity a few times and it's been transformative. Many of the difficulties we encounter in living a vegan lifestyle, for our families and ourselves, arise because we are basically alone in a culture that is hostile to our values. I found when I was immersed in large-scale vegan communities, contradictions and complications evaporated in a remarkable feeling of inner wholeness.

March 11

We will hopefully be able to create more and more opportunities for people to experience vegan community in North America and elsewhere. Practicing compassionate living together can send boundless waves of healing energy into our world and help awaken the slumbering conscience of our species.

March 12

As we practice leaving home by examining our own societal indoctrination and questioning all the propaganda continually spewed forth by the military-industrial-meat-medical complex, we can liberate ourselves and live a life of greater compassion based on vegan ethics and a plant-based diet, and be a voice for those vulnerable sentient creatures who have no voice. In this we fulfill the universal teachings that promote spiritual living. We are practicing compassion and making connections, and our life can become a field of freedom and love as we continually affirm our interdependence with all life, and practice non-cooperation with those forces that see beings as mere commodities.

March 13

Even though people may resist hearing it, spreading the vegan message is the greatest gift we can give, for it is ultimately liberating for everyone. With study and practice, we can articulate it skillfully, passionately, and effectively, and help other people to understand as well!

March 14

Every person who authentically goes vegan is a person who is rediscovering the lost chalice of intuitive wisdom, and by refusing to participate in the killing and enslaving of mothers and babies, and honoring the sacred dimension and reclaiming intuitive wisdom, is helping to transform our culture in profound and significant ways. As Goethe said, "To know is not enough. You must apply." Spiritual teachings emphasize that whatever we deeply desire we must first give to others. To recover the lost chalice, we are called to give the female animals we exploit the opportunity to express their maternal wisdom again.

March 15

Veganism is actually a spectrum of psychospiritual development, and the most basic level of veganism is refraining from buying foods and products that cause suffering to animals. As our veganism deepens, we realize that veganism is radical inclusion, and that it calls us to act with respect and kindness in all our relations with everyone, all the time. A tall order! In short, veganism is an ideal that is perhaps ultimately unattainable, but that draws us ever onward to greater love and compassion in every dimension of our lives.

March 16

Veganism is the natural flowering of consciousness freed from the continuous programming of the inherent violence in our culture. The word vegan is precious, inspiring, and demanding, because it questions the core mentality of our culture and it is the key to our culture's transformation and to its very survival. So please, let's love, defend, respect, understand, and propagate this word and what it stands for as if all our lives depended upon it; they very well may.

March 17

Corporations were created for one reason: to avoid responsibility; spirituality and veganism, if they are expressions of anything, are expressions of taking responsibility. In the big picture, we are all responsible for our treatment of others, as well as for our failures to act to help others. To finally solve the dilemma we see reflected in political corruption, we must cut the root of the problem, which is the herding mentality that commodifies animals and the weak and gives rise to the corporate worldview. Veganism is the only lasting solution.

March 18

Veganism, which is a committed effort to live the ideals of mercy and kindness to others, is indispensable to all spiritual paths, because it emerges from and deepens the understanding that all beings are completely interconnected and interdependent. It is an inclusive movement that advocates a plant-based diet because it includes all sentient creatures within its sphere of concern. The towering spiritual geniuses who have blessed this earth have typically been vegan but have been little concerned whether their foods were cooked or not. For example, when we look at the great Zen masters of China and East Asia of the last 1,500 years, we find people who invariably ate a vegan diet of both cooked and uncooked foods. The desert fathers of the Christian tradition are similar.

March 19

Veganism is the essential healing force that our culture desperately needs, because the mentality of domination that starts on our plates reverberates through our various cultural institutions as authoritarianism, oppression, and violence. Healing this mentality requires cultivating vegan values: concern and caring for others weaker than us, and refusing to exploit them. As vegans, the improved health we naturally experience is a side-benefit; it's not the main focus because we sense there's a higher purpose in life than just being physically healthy.

March 20

The secret to happiness and inner peace is thus not just the Law of Attraction and being mindful of our thoughts, although this is certainly important. The secret is being mindful of our actions as well, because just as our thoughts condition our behavior, our behavior conditions our thoughts, and regular daily actions of instigating violence and eating the results of that violence keep our consciousness and thoughts confined to a relatively low vibrational level.

March 21

The real secret to personal and planetary peace and happiness is veganism rightly understood as the ancient and timeless teaching to include all living beings within the sphere of our kindness and respect, and never to treat any being as a mere object to be used or abused. This is the awakening of our true human heart, not for a self-centered happiness, but for a happiness that includes everyone. This is positive thinking beyond mere positive thinking; it's living the truth that we are, and being the transformation we long to see in our world.

Now let's imagine that!—and live it.

March 22

When we come to this earth, we find ourselves in a culture that is at its very core organized around confining and killing animals for food. We are forced virtually from birth to look at beings as mere commodities and to treat them as such by eating them in the most powerful daily rituals we engage in: our meals. Fortunately, as we awaken and stop disconnecting from the suffering we cause others by our choices, we resensitize ourselves and begin to be a force for kindness and respect that can impact others, and we can work through our culture's institutions to raise consciousness and spread the light of inclusiveness. The more clearly the inner light shines in us, the more clearly we can shine it into the world.

March 23

Looking around, we can see the tremendous urgency in the task required of us: to do all we can to influence our culture to evolve and embrace the vegan ideals of interconnectedness, freedom, and caring. The same urgency is required in our inner lives as well. Going vegan is much more than minimizing the cruelty and suffering we cause others; it is awakening the heart of loving inclusiveness and realizing that there are, ultimately, no separate selves. We are all connected.

March 24

Each of us is radically and profoundly interconnected with all other living beings, and by blessing and encouraging and seeing the best in others, we help everyone, and by condemning or turning away from others, we harm everyone, including ourselves. Shining compassion to everyone, even our apparent opponents, is the essence of the benevolent revolution that is veganism.

March 25

Veganism is, I've found, a litmus test of religious teachings and religious teachers. To the degree that religious teachings do not explicitly encourage veganism, which is the practice of nonviolence and lovingkindness, to that same degree these teachings are hypocritical and disconnected from their spiritual source.

March 26

Since the decision to become a vegan is at its core an ethical one, spirituality, which is the foundation of ethics, must be the foundation of veganism as well. The spiritual element within us encourages us not to harm others, but to express love and practice compassion. Compassion brings the intuition of spiritual awareness into daily life as actions that serve to help and bless others. Veganism is clearly a vital expression of this compassion that springs from our felt sense of connectedness with others. While it may not necessarily be religious, at its core, veganism is spiritual, and it is an expression of love. It is a concrete way that we can all be lovers.

March 27

What goes around comes around. We must as a species stop the violence that is inherent in our meat habit. This should be of paramount importance for all religious movements and teachers. It is the call of spirituality. If our religions don't hear this call, we must revitalize them or create new ones that do.

March 28

From the viewpoint of its deepest and most eternal and universal teachings—to love God, and to love our neighbor as ourself—the Bible unequivocally condemns animal slavery just as it condemns human slavery. We must stop using the Bible to justify animal abuse, but rather use it to guide us in our quest for peace and justice for all beings.

March 29

As vegans, we may feel sad, bitter, misunderstood, and isolated by the apparently oblivious attitudes of our culture, friends, and families. What can we do? In a few words, we can cultivate a sense of joy and thankfulness. In the face of our culture's unrelenting pressure to view animals as mere food commodities, going vegan is a victory for peace, a real spiritual breakthrough.

March 30

As vegans, we're a force for healing and compassion every day and at every meal. Our way of living exemplifies mercy and promotes freedom, and offers opportunities to unfold wisdom and help heal our world. These are true causes for an abiding sense of joy. Even in the midst of grief and outrage at our culture's cruelty, we can be glad that our ability to feel is reawakening.

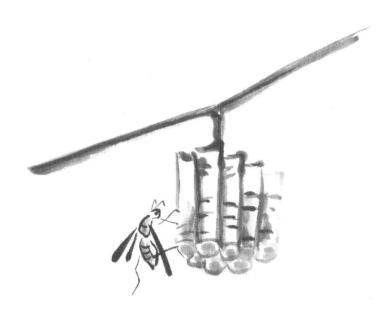

March 31

The act of regularly eating foods derived from confined and brutalized animals forces us to become somewhat emotionally desensitized, and this numbing and inner armoring make it possible for us as a culture to devastate the earth, slaughter people in wars, and support oppressive social structures without feeling remorse. By going vegan, we're taking responsibility for the effects of our actions on vulnerable beings and we're resensitizing ourselves. We're becoming more alive, and more able to feel both grief and joy. Kahlil Gibran points out in *The Prophet* that unless we are able to feel our grief and weep our tears, we will not be able to laugh our laughter, either. Turning our pain and outrage into action on behalf of vulnerable beings will bring healing to us and to our world.

April 1

The foundation of our culture's systemic violence against animals for food is a mentality of exclusion. For us as vegans to be a force for the revolution of compassion that is called for if our culture is to survive, we must heal the mentality of exclusion within ourselves, and exclude no one from our understanding and compassion. We don't have the luxury to cultivate anger, or allow it to be a motivation, because anger is a poison that is inherently exclusionary. We are called, as Gandhi said, to *be* the change we want to see. There is no motivation more revolutionary than joy-filled loving-kindness.

April 2

The revolution implicit in veganism is a revolution of universal love and inclusiveness and its energy of joy can wash the planet clean and transform ugly human folly. Give thanks every day for the joy in your heart and that you see reflected in the birds, flowers, trees, and in the whole web of celebrating life, for that is what you are.

April 3

Stay open and sensitive to the suffering of both animals and humans, and bring as much loving-kindness as you can to all your relationships with others, including yourself. We are all connected, and your joy brings joy to others and makes your veganism more appealing and contagious to others.

April 4

Fish absorb and intensely concentrate toxins like PCBs, dioxins, radioactive substances, and heavy metals like mercury, lead, cadmium, and arsenic, all of which are linked to cancer as well as nervous system disorders, kidney damage, and impaired mental functioning. They contain excessive amounts of cholesterol, animal protein, and hazardous, blood-altering oils. Besides contributing directly to human disease and suffering through the toxicity of its products, the seafood industry causes enormous damage to marine ecosystems throughout the world.

April 5

The essence of the mentality that allows us to confine and kill animals for food is the mentality of exclusion. We are all taught by our culture from infancy to exclude certain beings from the sphere of our compassion. Veganism is a radical response to this: it is a mentality of utter inclusion: we consciously practice including all living beings within our circle of caring; we exclude no one. Anger is an expression of exclusion. It destroys veganism and compassion. We are called, as vegans, to transform our anger toward those who are harming animals, people, the Earth, and future generations into compassion and understanding for them.

April 6

It is illuminating to look at our treatment of animals and see how our mistreatment of them has painful repercussions for us. The ironies involved are remarkable. For example, animals in the wild are never fat, but animals raised for food are severely confined and fed special diets and given drugs and hormones in order to make them unnaturally fat. They're sold by the pound, after all. Sowing obesity in billions of animals we reap it in ourselves.

April 7

We are taught as children to practice certain ways of seeing the world and of relating to others, and we gradually become adept in these practices. In our culture, we are taught to practice disconnecting the reality of animal flesh and secretions in our meals from the actual reality of the animal cruelty required to get them onto our plates. Going vegan is a commitment to practice something else, to practice in a completely different way than we were taught by our culture. Instead of practicing desensitizing, disconnecting, and reducing others, we practice reconnecting, resensitizing ourselves, and respecting others. This commitment comes from deep within us, from our inherent compassion and our inner urge to evolve spiritually and to live with awareness, kindness, freedom, and joy.

April 8

Practicing veganism means practicing respect and sensitivity toward others, especially those who are vulnerable and without social privilege, and is precisely the practice required to bring healing to our corrupt and wounded culture. Veganism is a call to renounce the core practice of our culture—reducing beings to mere harvestable and abuseable commodities—and to practice, in every aspect of our lives, its opposite: mindfulness, inclusiveness, equality, and respect.

April 9

The power of veganism is that it's *practiced*. Being vegan is often difficult, not only because of the outer resistance we face, but even more because of the inner resistance we experience: our culture has planted its seeds of exclusivism and violence in us from the time of our birth, and a big part of our practice is to cultivate vegan attitudes of kindness and respect for everyone, even our so-called opponents. With this practice, we can plant seeds for a new world of peace and justice in our shared consciousness on this planet and realize and live the truth of our essential interconnectedness. Our path is our daily practice, both inwardly and outwardly, and as the old saying goes, "practice makes perfect."

April 10

Like other animals, we are not fundamentally physical beings; we are essentially consciousness. We are all expressions of the infinite creative mystery force that births and sustains the universes of manifestation, and our bodies and minds are sacred, as are the bodies and minds of all creatures. Like us, animals have feelings and yearnings; they nest, mate, hunger, and are the conscious subjects of their lives. They make every effort, as we do, to avoid pain and death and to do what brings them happiness and fulfillment.

April 11

The word vegan, newer and more challenging than the word vegetarian because it includes every sentient being in its circle of concern and addresses all forms of unnecessary cruelty from an essentially ethical perspective, points to an ancient idea that has been articulated for many centuries, especially in the world's spiritual traditions. It indicates a mentality of expansive inclusiveness and is able to embrace science and virtually all religions because it is a manifestation of the yearning for universal peace, justice, wisdom, and freedom.

April 12

The roots of our crises lie in our dinner plates. Our inherited food choices bind us to an obsolete mentality that inexorably undermines our happiness, intelligence, and freedom. Turning away is no longer an option. We are all related.

April 13

There is no force more subversive to our culture than practicing vegans, no force more challenging, healing, transformative, and uplifting than people living the truth that all life is sacred and interconnected.

April 14

Eating the flesh and secretions of animals is so fundamentally repulsive to us as humans that these animal foods make especially powerful placebos. We find vultures repulsive because they eat carrion, but we eat exactly the same thing! Sometimes it's euphemized as aged beef. And yet, because we've been taught to attribute strength and energy to eating animal foods, that expectation helps our quite miraculous and flexible psychophysiology to partially overcome the essentially disturbing and toxic nature of these foods so we can survive and function. As children, we had no other choice.

April 15
Animal foods require immense quantities of petroleum to produce. For example, while it takes only two calories of fossil fuel to produce one calorie of protein from soybeans, and three calories for wheat and corn, it takes fifty-four calories of petroleum to produce one calorie of protein from beef! Animal agriculture contributes disproportionately to our consumption of petroleum and thus to air and water pollution, global warming, and the wars driven by conflict over dwindling petroleum reserves.

April 16
Our body is our most precious friend. It works ceaselessly to maintain health and harmony and is our vehicle for expression and experience in this world. What could be more valuable and worthy of care and protection? It never works against us, but always does its best with whatever it has to work with. It is a shame that so many of these immeasurably valuable gifts from the loving source of all life, beautiful expressions of spiritual creativity, are distracted and harmed unnecessarily, saddled with heavy burdens that were never intended or foreseen by nature, and tragically destroyed by ignorance, fear, and a lack of caring. Radiant physical health is such a treasure; yet how rare it is today, particularly among those of us who abuse animals for food.

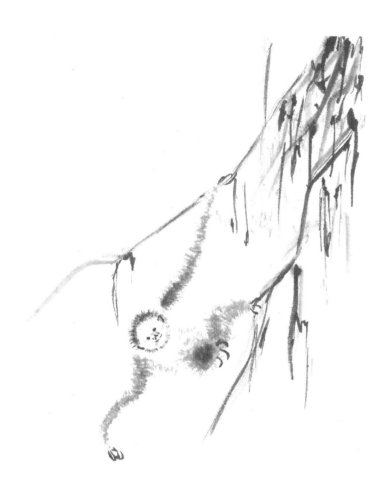

April 17

It's actually quite obvious why heart disease and cancer "run in the family." Everyone in the family has their legs under the same dinner table! As children we not only eat like our family but also soak up our inner attitudes from them. Unless we metaphorically leave home and question our culture's food mentality and the enslaving propaganda of the meat-medical complex, we will find it difficult to discern our unique mission and grow spiritually. Spiritual health, like physical and mental health, urges us to take responsibility for our lives, and to dedicate ourselves to a cause that is higher than our self-preoccupations.

April 18

The most solid and enduring motivations for action are ultimately based on caring for others—in this case imprisoned animals, wildlife, starving people, slaughterhouse workers, and future generations, to name some of those damaged by our desire for animal foods. The health advantages of a plant-based diet are the perquisites of loving-kindness and awareness, and the diseases and discomfort caused by animal foods are some of the consequences that follow from breaking natural laws.

April 19

We are all in this together. The vegan revolution will never include violence; it is a celebration of the joy and beauty of life, and an awakening to the beauty and potential of our shared life on this planet. The only strategy for each of us is how to love and give more deeply, fully, and authentically, and in harmony with our unique talents and gifts. Together, we are transforming our world!

April 20

Chefs know that fish who die with great resistance, struggling against the net or the hook and line, have a more bitter taste because of the lactic acid that remains in their muscles. In eating fish, we eat the lactic acid the fish produce in their death throes, and the fear-induced adrenalin and other hormones. We can all get ample high-quality protein from plant sources without causing unnecessary misery and trauma to other living creatures.

April 21

Eighty percent of grain grown in the U.S. and about half the fish hauled in are wasted to grow billions of animals big and fat enough to be profitably slaughtered, or to produce dairy products and eggs at the high levels demanded by consumers. And over ninety percent of the protein in this grain turns into the methane, ammonia, urea, and manure that pollutes our air and water. A conservative estimate is that the amount of land, grain, water, petroleum, and pollution required to feed one of us the Standard American Diet could feed fifteen of us eating a plant-based diet.

April 22

As far as taste goes, those of us who follow a plant-based diet invariably report that we discover new vistas of delicious foods that we hardly knew existed. Plant-based cuisines from the Mediterranean, Africa, India, East Asia, Mexico, and South America all offer delicious and nutritious possibilities. As our taste buds come back to life, we discover more subtle nuances of flavor, and as our hearts and minds relax and rejoice in supporting more cruelty-free foods, the foods become increasingly delicious. Due to the mind-body connection, they also become more nutritious as we begin to enjoy partaking of the attractive and regenerating fruits and herbs of our earth. Mindful eating is the essential foundation of happiness and peace.

April 23

As people learn more about the consequences of eating animal foods, we see increasing numbers of individuals and groups acting creatively to raise consciousness about this, thus helping to eliminate the roots of hunger, cruelty, pollution, and exploitation. Food Not Bombs, for example, organizes volunteers and food donations to feed disadvantaged hungry people organic vegan food in over 175 cities throughout the Americas, Europe, and Australia. It is intentionally decentralized and web-like in its approach, with autonomous local units organizing their own compassionate operations. The worldwide followers of Ching Hai, a noted Vietnamese spiritual teacher with students numbering in the hundreds of thousands, have set up vegan restaurants in many cities and contribute vegan food, clothing, shelter, and aid to disaster victims, prisoners, children, and the elderly in countries around the world. These are but two encouraging examples of the vegan revolution of compassion, justice and equality taking firmer root in our culture and in the world.

April 24

The ancient wisdom ever holds: Violence begets violence. As we sow, so shall we reap. Now is the time to sow seeds of understanding, patience, and inner reflection, and to truly live more simply, encourage a more plant-based diet, and work to transform our culture, with a view toward caring for all the humans on this beautiful earth, all the precious creatures here, and all those of the future generations who depend upon us to be responsible for our actions. As Gandhi said, "There is enough for everyone's need, but not for everyone's greed."

April 25

This is the wonderful news! Each and every one of us can help transform our culture in the most effective way possible: by switching to a plant-based diet for ethical reasons and encouraging others to do the same. This is veganism, which is a mentality and lifestyle of radical inclusion and compassion, and it is the antidote to our culture's sickness, going to the hidden root of our dilemmas. It is the beckoning revolution that will make peace, sustainability, and heaven actually possible on this Earth. Anyone can go vegan today and help transform our world with every meal. We can each be the change we want to see in the world and bring forth the benevolent transformation we all yearn for in our hearts.

April 26

The choice is set before us at every meal between the garden of life or the altar of death and as we choose life and eat grains and vegetables rather than flesh, milk, and eggs, we find our joy rising, our health increasing, our spirit deepening, our mind quickening, our feelings softening, and our creativity flourishing.

April 27

We can transform this culture we live in, and which lives in us, by transforming our own motivations and exemplifying this to others. We owe this to the animals. In the end, we are not separate from others, and we each have a critical piece to the great puzzle of cultural awakening to contribute, and our success and fulfillment depend on each of us discovering this piece and presenting it persistently. As Albert Schweitzer said, "One thing I know. The only ones among you who will find happiness are those who have sought, and found, how to serve."

April 28

From one grain spring hundreds, thousands, and millions of grains, each of which has the same potential. How do we respond to this existential exuberance of life bursting with more life? Our response depends on our food! Universally, we feel a sense of wonder and joy upon entering a lovingly tended organic garden. It exudes beauty, magic, delight, and blessedness, and we instinctively feel grateful and blessed in the presence of the gifts we receive so freely from forces that accomplish what we can never do: bring forth new life from seeds, roots, and stems. And universally, we are repulsed by the violence and sheer horror and ugliness that are always required to kill animals for food, and at a deep cultural level, we feel ashamed of our relentless violence against animals for our meals.

April 29

Because of herding animals, we have cast ourselves out of the garden into the rat race of competition and consumerism, ashamed of ourselves. It is this low self-esteem that drives the profits of corporations enriching themselves on our insatiable craving for gadgets, drugs, and entertainment to help us forget what we know in our hearts, and to cover over the moans of the animals entombed in our flesh.

April 30
By confining and killing animals for food, we have brought violence into our bodies and minds and disturbed the physical, emotional, mental, social, and spiritual dimensions of our selves in deep and intractable ways. Our meals require us to eat like predators and thus to see ourselves as such, cultivating and justifying predatory behaviors and institutions that are the antithesis of the inclusiveness and kindness that accompany spiritual growth.

May 1
Seeing our eating habits for what they are, and answering the call of our spirit to understand the consequences of our actions, we become open to compassion, intelligence, freedom, and to living the truth of our interconnectedness with all life.

May 2
Food is actually our most intimate and telling connection both with the natural order and with our living cultural heritage. Through eating the plants and animals of this earth we literally incorporate them, and it is also through this act of eating that we partake of our culture's values and paradigms at the most primal and unconscious levels.

May 3

By confining and killing animals for food, we have brought violence
into our bodies and minds and disturbed the physical, emotional,
mental, social and spiritual dimensions of ourselves in deep and
intractable ways.

May 4

As children, through constant exposure to the complex patterns of
belief surrounding our most elaborate group ritual, eating food, we
ingested our culture's values and invisible assumptions. Like sponges,
we learned, we noticed, we partook, and we became acculturated.

Now, as adults, finding our lives beset with stress and a range of daunting problems of our own making, we rightly yearn to understand the source of our frustrating inability to live in harmony on this earth.

May 5
Until we are willing and able to make the connections between what we are eating and what was required to get it on our plate, and how it affects us to buy, serve, and eat it, we will be unable to make the connections that will allow us to live wisely and harmoniously on this Earth.

May 6
Eating animal foods is a fundamental cause of our dilemmas, but we will squirm every which way to avoid confronting this. It is our defining blind spot and is the essential missing piece to the puzzle of human peace and freedom.

May 7
Our behavior invariably reflects our understanding, and yet our behavior also determines what level of understanding we are able to attain.

May 8
The calling we hear today is the persistent call to evolve. It is part of a larger song to which we all contribute and that lives in our cells and in the essential nature of the universe that gives rise to our being. It is a song, ultimately, of healing, joy, and celebration because all of us, humans and non-humans alike, are expressions of a beautiful and benevolent universe. It is also a song of darkest pain and violation, due to our accepted practices of dominating, commodifying, and killing animals and people.

May 9

In order to confine and kill animals for food, we must repress our natural compassion, warping us away from intuition and toward materialism, violence, and disconnectedness

May 10

The song of the new mythos that yearns to be born through us requires our spirits to be loving and alive enough to hear and recognize the pain we are causing through our obsolete food orientation. We are called to allow our innate mercy and kindness to shine forth and to confront the indoctrinated assumptions that promote cruelty.

May 11

The inner feminine is our intuition, our sensitivity, and our ability to sense the profound interconnectedness of events and beings, and it is vital to peace, wisdom, joy, intelligence, creativity, and spiritual awakening. With every baby calf stolen from her mother and killed, with every gallon of milk stolen from enslaved and broken mothers, with every thrust of the raping sperm gun, with every egg stolen from a helpless, frantic hen, and with every baby chick killed or locked for life in a hellish nightmare cage, we kill the sacred feminine within ourselves.

May 12

Food is not only a fundamental necessity; it is also a primary symbol in the shared inner life of every human culture, including our own. It is not hard to see that food is a source and metaphor of life, love, generosity, celebration, pleasure, reassurance, acquisition, and consumption. And yet it is also, ironically, a source and metaphor of control, domination, cruelty, and death, for we often kill to eat.

May 13

Looking deeply into food, into what and how we eat, and into the attitudes, actions, and beliefs surrounding food, is an adventure of looking into the very heart of our culture and ourselves. As surprising as it may seem, as we shine the light of awareness onto this most ordinary and necessary aspect of our lives, we shine light onto unperceived chains of bondage attached to our bodies, minds, and hearts, onto the bars of cages we never could quite see, and onto a sparkling path that leads to transformation and the possibility of true love, freedom, and joy in our lives.

May 14

Eating is the most intimate of all activities in which we actually accomplish the complex and longed-for union of self and other, subject and world. And so it has always been seen, cross-culturally, as the most sacred human activity, and the most culturally binding as well.

May 15

Though it appears that we are mere finite beings eating food, from another perspective we can see the infinite eternally feeding itself with itself. Through this act of partaking, we open, embrace, and actually embody the infinite order as a unique expression of itself, which is us, these human beings who are eating. This is an expression of the profoundest love.

May 16

Animal-based meals are the source of the complacency and sense of disempowerment that permit the environmental and social holocaust that our media prevents us from seeing and comprehending. Eating animal foods diminishes our sensitivity, paralyzing us by reducing our ability to respond—our response-ability. Eating the violence on our plates requires an evasion of responsibility so that we come to believe our actions don't make much difference. This erroneous belief is actually rooted in our semi-conscious understanding that with every meal we cause exactly the kind of suffering and pollution that we would naturally want to prevent.

May 17

A plant-based diet cannot be patented, so it is of absolutely no interest to the pharmaceutical complex. It is an enormous threat, in fact, and huge campaigns are waged to keep us distracted and believing that complex carbohydrates are bad for us while animal protein is absolutely necessary, and that science can save us from diabetes, cancer, and the other diseases brought on by our callous domination of animals for food.

May 18

Billions are spent searching for drugs and other material means to cure what is actually an ethical and spiritual disease. Sowing disease and death in animals at our mercy, we reap the same in ourselves.

May 19

Our lives flow from our beliefs, and our beliefs are conditioned by our daily actions. As we act, so we build our character and so we become. By consciously making our meals celebrations of peace, compassion, and freedom, we can sow seeds in the most powerful way possible to contribute to the healing of our world.

May 20

Eating food is a lot like sex in that the inner images and attitudes we have are more important to our enjoyment than the physical or objective reality of which or of whom we partake. Our taste is determined, ultimately, by our mind.

May 21

Another reason plant-based foods taste better is that we feel better eating them and contemplating their origins. Eating slowly, we enjoy contemplating the organic orchards and gardens that supply the delicious vegetables, fruits, and grains we're eating.

May 22

We grow to appreciate the nearly miraculous beauty of cabbages and cauliflower, the fragrance of roasted sesame seeds, sliced oranges, chopped cilantro, and baked kabocha squash, and the wondrous textures of avocado, persimmon, steamed quinoa, and sautéed tempeh. We are grateful for the connection we feel with the earth, the clouds, the nurturing gardeners, and the seasons, and the tastes are delicious gifts we naturally enjoy opening to, as we would open to our beloved in making love and appreciating the beloved fully. In contrast, eating animal foods is often done quickly, without feeling deeply into the source of the food—for who would want to contemplate the utter hells that produce our factory-farmed fish, chicken, eggs, cheese, steaks, bacon, hot dogs, or burgers?

May 23

When we contemplate our tastes, we can see how conditioned they actually are. More importantly, though, we can see how utterly unsupportable they are as reasons to commit violence against defenseless, feeling beings. Self-centered craving for pleasure and fulfillment at the expense of others is the antithesis of the Golden Rule and of every standard of morality.

May 24

Since our culture denies animals used for food any inherent value in their own right, limiting their worth simply to their value as commodities to those who own them, animals have no protection. Ordering a steak earns us approving nods, and our friends rave over the barbecued ribs at the office picnic. The actual confinement, raping, mutilating, and killing are kept carefully hidden as shameful secrets that would make us profoundly uncomfortable if we had to witness them or, worse, perform them ourselves.

May 25

We can see that the three reasons that we eat animal foods—infant indoctrination, social and market pressure, and taste—reinforce each other and create a force field around our food choices that, like a sturdy fortress, resists any incursions. The walls of the fortress are built of cruelty, denial, ignorance, force, conditioning, and selfishness. Most importantly, they are not of our choosing. They have been, and are being, forced upon us. Our well-being—and our survival—depend on our seeing this clearly and throwing off our chains of domination and unawareness. By harming and exploiting billions of animals, we confine ourselves spiritually, morally, emotionally, and cognitively, and blind ourselves to the poignant, heart-touching beauty of nature, animals, and each other.

May 26

To be free, we must practice freeing others. To feel loved, we must practice loving others. To have true self-respect, we must respect others. The animals and other voiceless beings, the starving humans and future generations, are pleading with us to see: it's on our plate.

May 27

Ending obesity will remain difficult, mysterious, complex, and a losing battle as long as we continue to eat diets rich in high-fat animal flesh, eggs, and dairy products.

May 28

Albert Einstein was correct in saying that no problem can be solved at the level on which it was created. As omnivores, we must go to another level to solve our problem with excess fat, a level where we no longer kill and confine animals by proxy and consume their fat-laden remains.

May 29

It is well known that animal foods are heavily contaminated with viruses and bacteria such as salmonella, listeria, E. coli, campylobacter, and streptococcus, which can be harmful if not fatal to people, especially given our already overworked immune systems. The urea in animal flesh also contains toxins. It has furthermore recently been shown that cooked animal flesh contains heterocyclic amines, which are carcinogenic chemicals that form during the cooking process. Thus, by not cooking flesh enough, we may expose ourselves to salmonella, E. coli, and other pathogens, and by cooking it, we end up eating cancer-causing chemicals formed by heating the animal fat.

May 30

Looking from a variety of perspectives at our animal-based meals, we discover that eating animals has consequences far beyond what we would at first suspect. Like a little boy caught tormenting frogs, our culture mumbles, "It's no big deal," and looks away. And yet the repercussions of our animal-based diet are a very big deal indeed, not only for the unfortunate creatures in our hands, but for us as well.

May 31

Even those who acknowledge that our treatment of animals is indeed a great evil may feel that it is, like the other evils in our world, simply a product of human limitations, such as ignorance, pride, selfishness, fear, and so forth. According to this view, the horror we inflict on animals is a problem, but not a fundamental *cause* of our problems— and, because it's a problem for animals, who are less important than us humans, it's a lesser problem.

June 1

If we fail to make the connection between our daily meals and our cultural predicament, we will inevitably fail as a species to survive on this earth. By refusing to make this essential connection, we condemn others and ourselves to enormous suffering, without ever comprehending why.

June 2

We become a revolution of one, contributing to the foundation of a new world with every meal we eat. As we share our ideas with others, we promote what may be the most uplifting and healing revolution our culture has ever experienced.

June 3

The fat we carry around under our skin is mainly the fat of miserable and terrified animals—it's not surprising we're anxious to be rid of it! If we based our diet on the whole grains, fruits, vegetables and legumes for which we are designed, we would find the obesity problem in our culture evaporating, along with many other problems.

June 4

Perpetrators and victims are known to exchange roles over and over again in countless subtle and obvious ways. The cycle of violence may span larger dimensions than we in our herding culture would like to admit, and there are many wisdom traditions that affirm that it does. Until we see from the highest level, we had best heed the counsel of every enlightened spiritual teacher from every time: be ye kind to one another.

June 5

We have all been given the gift of physical bodies that require no animal to suffer for their feeding. However, we've all been conditioned from infancy by our culture to reject this gift, and to unnecessarily confine, slaughter, and eat animals, and this sows the seeds of generations of misery.

June 6

The human cycle of violence will not stop until we stop the *underlying* violence, the remorseless violence we commit against animals for food. We teach this behavior and this insensitivity to all our children in a subtle, unintentional, but powerful form of culturally approved child abuse.

June 7

Our actions condition our consciousness; therefore forcing our children to eat animal foods wounds them deeply. It requires them to disconnect from the food on their plates, from their feelings, from animals and nature, and sets up conditions of disease and psychological armoring. The wounds persist and are passed on to the next generation.

June 8

Compelling our children to eat animal foods gives birth to the "hurt people hurt people" syndrome. Hurt people hurt animals without compunction in daily food rituals. We will always be violent toward each other as long as we are violent toward animals—how could we not be? We carry the violence in our stomachs, in our blood, and in our consciousness. Covering it up and ignoring it doesn't make it disappear. The more we pretend and hide it, the more, like a shadow, it clings to us and haunts us. The human cycle of violence is the ongoing projection of this shadow.

June 9

There is an enormously positive revolution implicit in this effort to understand the consequences of our food choices: a spiritual transformation that can potentially launch our culture into a quantum evolutionary leap, from emphasizing consumption, domination, and self-preoccupation to nurturing creativity, liberation, inclusion, and cooperation.

June 10

The ripples that radiate from our choices to eat foods from animal sources are incredibly far-reaching and complex. They extend deeply into our essential orientation and belief system, and into our relationships with each other and the created order. From every perspective we can possibly take, we discover that our culturally imposed eating habits are numbing, blinding, and confining us.

June 11

The spiritual and cultural revolution that calls us must begin with our food. Food is our primary connection with the earth and her mysteries, and with our culture. It is the foundation of economy and is the central inner spiritual metaphor of our lives.

June 12

Even if we are benumbed to the degree that we are not concerned about the suffering of animals, and we are only able to care about other humans, we soon realize that the human anguish caused by eating foods of animal origin requires us to choose a plant-based diet. Human starvation, the emotional devastation required to kill and confine animals, the pollution and waste of water, land, petroleum, and other vital resources, and the injustice and violence underlying our animal food production complex all compel us to abandon our acculturated eating habits.

June 13

The inner action of leaving home necessitates in many ways a spiritual breakthrough. The essential action is to stop turning away and disconnecting from the suffering we impose on others by our food choices.

June 14

Once a vegan, we are always so, because our motivation is not personal and self-oriented, but is based on concern for others and on our undeniable interconnectedness with other living beings.

June 15

Actually, the taste that we prize in animal foods is more like the sex we would have as rapists, for the prostitute may at least consent and profit from our cravings, but the animal is always forced against her will to be tortured and killed for our taste and questionable pleasure.

June 16

The urge to show mercy and to protect those who are vulnerable is rooted deeply in us, and though it has been repressed by our herding culture, there is enormous evidence that it longs to be expressed by virtually all of us. We will collectively donate millions of dollars, for example, to help just one animal if we know the animal's story and our intelligence and compassion have been awakened by our connecting with this animal.

June 17

The more we connect, the more we understand and the more we love, and this love propels us not only to leave home, questioning our culture's attitude of domination and exclusion, but also to return home, speaking on behalf of those who are vulnerable.

June 18

The opposite of love is not hate but indifference. When we lift the veil and see the suffering our food habits cause, when we connect with the reality of the defenseless beings who suffer so terribly because of our food choices, our indifference dissolves and compassion—its opposite—arises, urging us to act on behalf of those who are suffering.

June 19

A primary danger is that we might leave home but not return; that is, we could awaken to the harmfulness inherent in our culture's commodification of living beings but fail to bring this awakening to our culture by becoming a voice for these beings. If our understanding isn't articulated in ways that are meaningful for us, it can become imprisoned within us and turn sour, becoming cynicism, anger, despair, and disease. This doesn't serve us or anyone else.

June 20

When we cannot make connections, we cannot understand, and we are less free, less intelligent, less loving, and less happy. The most crucial task for our generation, our group mission on this earth, perhaps, is to make some essential connections that our parents and ancestors have been mostly unable to make, and thus to evolve a healthier human society to bequeath to our children.

June 21

We all have unique gifts we can bring to the most urgent task we face at this point in our human evolution: transforming our inherited dominator mentality by liberating those we have enslaved for food. The crucial elements are adopting a vegan lifestyle, educating ourselves, cultivating our spiritual potential, and plugging in to help educate others.

June 22

When, as vegans, we become sensitized to the violence of the food system, we can also see that omnivores are victims of this food system as well.

June 23

In violent crimes committed publicly, there are three roles acted out: that of the perpetrator, that of the victim, and that of the bystander. It is well known that perpetrators hope bystanders will be silent and look the other way so they can successfully continue their hurtful actions, and that victims hope the bystanders will speak up, act, get involved, and do something to stop or discourage perpetrators from their harmful actions. With regard to eating animal foods, there are many perpetrators and victims and just a few bystanders. The perpetrators always encourage each other and regard the bystanders with suspicion and hostility, and the victims' voices cannot be heard.

June 24

Are we ready for a spiritual revolution? If we refuse, the strife, stress, and destruction will almost certainly intensify due to our ascending numbers and exploitive technology. When is a caterpillar ready to transform? The most obvious sign is the passing of its voracious appetite because an inner urge turns its attention to new directions.

June 25

To meditate for world peace, to pray for a better world, and to work for social justice and environmental protection while continuing to purchase the flesh, milk, and eggs of horribly abused animals exposes a disconnect that is so fundamental that it renders our efforts absurd, hypocritical, and doomed to certain failure.

June 26

Though we are born into a culture that emphasizes our differences from other animals, our actual experience tells us differently. Those of us with companion animals, for example, know without doubt that they have distinct personalities and preferences, emotions and drives, and that they feel and avoid psychological and physical pain.

June 27

The guilt and shame perpetrators feel for their violent actions stem from their natural sense of kindness and caring, which they have blocked and are violating. Their attitude toward bystanders may even be indignation: "If you want to be a vegetarian, that's fine, but don't tell us what to do." While at first blush this seems reasonable, we quickly see that it is only because of the disconnections and bias inherent in our culture. Perpetrators wouldn't dare say, "If you don't want to beat and stab your pet dog, that's fine, but don't tell me not to beat and stab mine." We all recognize that we aren't entitled to treat others, especially those who are defenseless, however we like, and that if we are responsible for doing harm, people have every right to ask us to stop.

June 28
Cultivating awareness is essential to realizing happiness, peace, and freedom.

June 29
Besides the enormous amount of anecdotal evidence that animals behave altruistically, both toward members of their own species and also to animals outside their species, there is clinical evidence as well, such as the typically cruel experiments in which monkeys were given food if they administered painful shocks to other monkeys. Researchers found that the monkeys would rather go hungry than shock other monkeys, especially if they had received shocks earlier themselves. The researchers were surprised (and perhaps somewhat ashamed?) by the monkeys' altruism. Though it is our true nature, one wonders if we humans would be so noble.

June 30
The bystander offers an example of nonviolence and speaks on behalf of the victims who have no voice (and, on a subtler level, on behalf of the perpetrators who are also victimized by their own actions). Perpetrators may condemn bystanders for judging them and making them feel bad or guilty, but the bystanders are merely acting as the

perpetrators' conscience, asking them to please become more aware and stop their violence, for everyone's sake.

July 1

As perpetrators, we are profoundly challenged by the truth-field established by attentive and articulate bystanders. Eventually, we may respond to the challenge, examine our attitudes and, recognizing our behavior as morally indefensible, cease it and join the ranks of the bystanders. As bystanders, we are also deeply challenged to respond creatively to the situation with love, understanding, and skillful means, and to strive to live in ever more complete alignment with the values of compassion, honesty, and integrity.

July 2

It's illustrative to watch how the attributes we have proclaimed make us unique, such as using tools, making art, experiencing "higher" emotions, having a sense of the ludicrous, using language, and so forth, have all collapsed under the evidence as we get to know animals better. Of course, we have certain unique attributes and abilities. *Every* species has certain unique attributes and abilities. Eating animals makes us so subconsciously nervous that we neurotically overemphasize our uniqueness and our separateness from them. This allows us to exclude them from our circle of concern.

July 3

Besides sharing a common home on this beautiful planet here in outer space, animals share with us the vulnerability of mortality and all that entails.

July 4

As food production industries brought their herds and flocks indoors into concentration camps, the extreme form of herding known as factory farming emerged. A new extreme form of factory farming is now emerging through genetic engineering, in which the animals are being tampered with at the genetic level, thus losing their biological integrity and identity. This is coupled with unparalleled destruction of habitat for wild animals and decimation of their populations for bush meat, pharmaceuticals, research, entertainment, and other human uses. Animals have thus gone from being free from human interference to being occasionally hunted, to being herded, to being imprisoned, and finally to being either forced into extinction or genetically mutated and confined as mere patentable property objects for human use.

July 5

It seems we're still so benighted as a culture that we'll refrain from committing violence only if we fear punishment or retaliation—and since animals are incapable of either, they have no protection from us at all.

July 6

Heavens and hells are of our own sowing. We live in a culture that mindlessly exploits animals and encourages the domination of those who are vulnerable by the strong, the male, the wealthy, and the privileged. This culture has naturally created political, economic, legal, religious, educational, and other institutional vehicles to shield those in power from the effects of their actions, and to legitimize the violence and inequities required to maintain the system. Over the centuries it has developed an elaborate scientific and religious framework that in its reductionism and materialism denies the continuity of consequences in many ways.

July 7

Because of our culturally inherited behavior of abusing the animals we use for food and ignoring this abuse, we are exceedingly hesitant to look behind the curtain of our denial, talk with each other about the consequences of our meals, and change our behavior to reflect what we see and know. This unwillingness is socially supported and continually reinforced.

July 8

The underlying assumptions of the culture into which we have been born are faulty and obsolete. If not questioned and changed, they will continue to drive us into deeper cultural insanity, just as they do the animals we mercilessly dominate.

July 9

As non-vegans, we are challenged by our spiritual and ethical disconnection to slow down, stop, pay attention, reconnect, embrace our disowned shadow, and begin the healing process. As vegans, we are challenged by our inconsistencies and fear of reprisal to pay attention and deepen our healing and awakening process by making the effort to align our thoughts, words, and actions with our understanding of interbeing and to ever more fully embody peace and courageous love.

July 10

While we are granted varying degrees of privilege depending on our species, race, class, and gender, we are all harmed when any is harmed; suffering is ultimately completely interconnected because we are all interconnected, and socially-constructed privilege only serves to disconnect us from this truth of our interdependence.

July 11

A positive momentum is unquestionably building in spite of the established forces of domination and violent control that would suppress it. Like a birth or metamorphosis, a new mythos is struggling through us to arise and replace the obsolete herding mythos, and the changes occurring may be far larger and more significant than they appear to be. They are ignored and discounted by the mass media, but what may seem to be small changes can suddenly mushroom when critical mass is reached.

July 12

Wealth, gender, and race determine the extent of our privilege in a human hierarchy between rich white men on one end and impoverished non-white women and children on the other. Even poor humans have some privilege compared to animals, however, and it is this hierarchical, authoritarian social structure—pervasive, transparent, and taken for granted—that is the unavoidable outcome of commodifying animals and eating them.

July 13

One particularly glaring inconsistency that should be further investigated is the underlying assumption of vivisection, that we can become healthier by destroying the health of other living beings. Our welfare is tied to the welfare of all beings; we cannot reap health in ourselves by sowing seeds of disease and death in others.

July 14

By including animals within the circle of relevant beings that we harm with our actions, we can get to the root of the destructive addictions that plague people in our culture. This is not to imply that all patterns of addictive behavior will necessarily disappear with the adoption of a vegan orientation to living, but it is a powerful start; inner weeding, mindfulness, and cultivating inner silence, patience, generosity, and gratitude are also essential dimensions of spiritual health.

July 15

If we decrease our practice of exploiting animals for food, we will find our levels of disease, mental illness, conflict, and environmental and social devastation likewise decreasing. Rather than ravaging the earth's body and decimating and incarcerating her creatures, we can join with the earth and be a force for creating beauty and spreading love, compassion, joy, peace, and celebration.

July 16

When we look with a relaxed eye at nature, we see an absolutely irrepressible celebration of living beauty. Animals in nature are both celebratory and inscrutable. They play, sing, run, soar, leap, call, dance, swim, hang out together, and relate in endlessly mysterious ways.

July 17

There is the macrobiotic perspective that animal foods are extremely yang in their energetic impact on the body, contracting the energy field, and that the body will then naturally and inevitably crave foods and substances that are extremely yin and expansive. These extreme yin foods are alcohol, white sugar, drugs of most every kind, tobacco, and caffeine. Grains, legumes, and vegetables tend to be neither excessively yin nor yang, but are more balanced, and so create few cravings. Eating extreme foods forces the body to gyrate continuously between the two poles, alternatively craving contracting foods like meat, cheese, eggs, and salt, and then expansive substances like sweets, coffee, alcohol, drugs, and tobacco, ad nauseam.

July 18

Freeing animals, we humans will be able to rejoin the celebration and contribute to it with our love and creativity. Competition and exploitation of other people can melt away as we regain our natural sensitivity.

July 19

As our culture adopts veganism, the change in our consciousness will usher in the first revolution since the herding revolution began with the domestication of sheep and goats 10,000 years ago. That revolution propelled us out of the garden into an existential sense of separateness, promoting competition and the cultivation of disconnected reductionism and materialistic technology. The evolutionary thrust is obviously now in a completely different direction, toward integration, cooperation, compassion, inclusiveness, and discovering our basic unity with all life.

July 20

The message ritually injected into us by our culturally mandated meals is, at a fundamental level, the message of privilege. As humans, we see ourselves as superior to animals, whom we view as objects to be enslaved and killed for our use and pleasure, and with this herder mentality of our special and privileged position over animals, we inevitably create other categories of privilege.

July 21
The wealthy elite exerts its privilege and authority through all our social institutions, using food as a method of maintaining control. By controlling food and disseminating junk food and food sourced from animals, those with the most privilege can confuse and sicken our entire population, especially those who are most vulnerable and uninformed. There are well-documented connections, for example, between the deterioration of our food supply and certain newly invented pathologies like attention deficit disorder.

July 22
By refusing to dominate animals, we make the essential connections and open inner doorways to understanding and deconstructing the abuse of privilege in our own lives. Justice, equality, veganism, freedom, spiritual evolution, and universal compassion are inextricably connected.

July 23
As long as we dominate others, we will be dominated.

July 24

Even those at the top of pyramid, the rich white men who have the most privilege, are ironically enslaved. Planting seeds of fear and domination, they cannot reap inner peace, joy, love, and happiness. The misery, drug addiction, suicide, and insanity rampant among the wealthiest families illustrate the obvious and inescapable truth that we are all related, and spiritual health, our source of happiness, requires us to live this truth in our daily lives.

July 25

Is there adequate time for us as a human family to make the transition to compassionate vegan living? It's a matter of education and reaching critical mass. Every one of us has an essential part to play in this greatest of all tasks.

July 26

While it's easy to become discouraged in the face of the immense cultural inertia that propels the continued practice of eating animal foods, it's helpful to realize that it carries within it the seeds of its own destruction. At the rate it's ravaging our planet's ecosystems and resources—and our sanity and intelligence—it cannot last much longer. These may very well turn out to be humanity's last days of eating animals.

July 27

To awaken from the cultural trance of omnivorism we need only remember who we are. We have neither the psychology nor the physiology for predation and killing, but due to the culturally indoctrinated mentality required by our daily meals, we eat like predators. We become desensitized, exclusivist and materialistic, forgetting that we are essentially consciousness manifesting in time and space. As consciousness, we are eternal, free, and benevolent.

July 28

When we are drawn toward a plant-based way of eating, it is in no way a limitation on us; rather it is the harmonious fulfillment of our own inner seeing. At first we think it's an option we can choose, but with time we realize that it's not a choice at all but the free expression of the truth that we are. It is not an ethic that we have to police from outside, but our own radiant love spontaneously expressing, both for ourselves and for our world. Caring is born on this earth and lives through us, as us, and it's not anything for which we can personally take credit. It is nothing to be proud of.

July 29

We are interconnected with all other manifestations of consciousness, and at a deep level we are all united because we share the same source. This source is the infinite intelligence and consciousness that permeates and manifests as phenomenal reality.

July 30

To free the animals we are abusing, we must free ourselves from the delusion of essential separateness, doing both the outer work of educating, sharing, and helping others, and the inner work of uncovering our true nature.

July 31

Metaphorically, we are all part of the movie of life on earth, and while we may appear to be the images on the screen, at a deeper level we share a common heritage—we are all also the light that makes the movie possible. This light is consciousness, and it is our fundamental nature, emanating from an infinite and inconceivable source.

August 1

Recognizing that we are all profoundly related, the greatest blessing we can give others, both animal and human, is to see their beauty, innocence, and uprightness, and address that in them.

August 2

In our culture, which is so permeated by the mentality of domination and exclusion, veganism requires a spiritual breakthrough. This breakthrough cannot be forced in any way by others, but it can definitely be encouraged.

August 3

The world we see is a product of our thoughts and way of seeing. Looking deeply into the animal-derived food on our plates, we see enormous suffering, abusive hands, and hardened hearts. Looking more deeply, we see that these hands and hearts have themselves been abused and wounded but yearn to be comforted and loved, and to comfort and love. As we see that abusers have always been abused themselves, we seek less to judge and more to understand, and to protect the vulnerable from abuse.

August 4

As we heal our wounds and stop eating animal foods we become better able to contribute to the healing of our culture. We see that we need less to be the hands of judgment and punishment—for pain willfully inflicted is unavoidably received again in the fullness of time—but rather to be the hands of mercy, help, and healing.

August 5

As we realize our interconnectedness with all living beings, our purpose naturally becomes to help and bless others, and it is a role we can carry without burnout or anger. The terrible suffering we see may certainly disturb and outrage us, but the outrage turns to compassion and creativity rather than to anger, despair, or vindictiveness.

August 6

By creating an inner field of peace, kindness, joy, and unity, we contribute to building a planetary field of compassion that reflects this consciousness.

August 7

As we hold steadfastly to the truth of being, knowing that compassion is irresistible and that it encircles the Earth through us and many others, and as we live this understanding in our daily lives and share it with others, we create a field of kindness and sow seeds of cultural transformation. There are no enemies because we are all related.

August 8

The spiritual connection between animals and humans grows out of understanding that we are all expressions of eternal benevolent consciousness, and as we acknowledge this interconnection and live in harmony with it, our lives become prayers of compassion and healing.

August 9

Just as waves are manifestations of the ocean and inseparable from it, we are both the light that makes the movie possible and the images on the screen illuminated by that light, each of us unique and contributing our voice, passion, and spirit to the unfolding story. With this understanding, we can live to help and bless others with both a sense of urgency, which is required and appropriate, and a sense of spaciousness that doesn't blame others or fight with them. Blaming and fighting only generate resistance and reinforce the delusion of separateness.

August 10

By ordering and eating products from the industrial herding complex that dominates the feminine with an iron fist, we squelch our opportunities for maturing to higher levels of understanding, sensitivity, and compassion. We remain merely ironic in our quests.

August 11

Our human spiritual evolution is a calling to liberate ourselves and the animals we hold in bondage. It's founded upon recognizing the unity of cause and effect: whatever seeds we sow in our consciousness we will reap in our lives. The ancient teaching holds true: "Hatred ceases not by hatred, but by love. This is the everlasting law." In the end, as Mahatma Gandhi emphasized, we must be the change we want to see in the world.

August 12

The most powerful antidotes to cruelty, abuse, and indifference are not anger and sadness, but love, peace, joy, and openhearted creative enthusiasm for this precious gift of a human life. Just as Thich Nhat Hanh has wisely said that without inner peace, we cannot contribute to the peace movement, so it is also that without inner freedom, we cannot contribute to the liberation of animals, which is the essential prerequisite to meaningful human freedom.

August 13

Veganism kindles a deep sense of peace in nature and of kinship, fellowship, and harmony with all life. It encourages a sense of inner richness that keeps growing and deepening as years go by, a sense of gentleness and of purpose.

August 14

Becoming vegan is not so much a decision made with our intellect as it is a natural consequence of inner ripening. While it's certainly helpful to comprehend intellectually the vast mandala of negative consequences of eating animal foods, we find that we are propelled into veganism by our intuition. As our intuitive heart opens, it opens to understanding our connection with others and to including them within the sphere of our concern.

August 15

Looking behind the curtain to the horrific suffering inherent in animal foods, asking questions, contemplating spiritual teachings, cultivating the higher knowing of intuition, and observing the example of other vegans all contribute to the ripening process. Once we can clearly see the universal law or principle underlying veganism, we can experience a spiritual transformation that allows greater possibilities of freedom and happiness.

August 16

Once we see and understand, we become a voice for the voiceless, a note in the glorious chord of healing and awakening that is endlessly unfolding in our shared consciousness.

August 17

Our inherited meal traditions require a mentality of violence and denial that silently radiates into every aspect of our private and public lives, permeating our institutions and generating the crises, dilemmas, inequities, and suffering that we seek in vain to understand and effectively address. A new way of eating no longer based on privilege, commodification, and exploitation is not only possible but essential and inevitable. Our innate intelligence demands it.

August 18

Every day, from the cradle to the grave, we all make food choices, or they are made for us. The quality of awareness from which these inevitable food choices arise—and whether we are making them ourselves or they are being made for us—greatly influences our ability to make connections. This ability to make meaningful connections determines whether we are and become lovers and protectors of life or unwitting perpetuators of cruelty and death.

August 19

As our hearts open to deeper understanding, our circle of compassion naturally enlarges and spontaneously begins to include more and more "others"—not just our own tribe, sect, nation, or race, but all human beings, and not just humans, but other mammals, and birds, fish, forests, and the whole beautifully interwoven tapestry of living, pulsing creation. All beings. All of Us.

August 20

Refraining from eating and using animals is the natural result of seeing that is no longer chained within the dark and rigid dungeon of narrow self-interest.

August 21

From the outside, it may look like and be called "veganism," but it is simply awareness and the expression of our sense of interconnectedness. It manifests naturally as inclusiveness and caring. It's no big deal, for it's the normal functioning of our original nature, which unfailingly sees beings rather than things when it looks at our neighbors on this Earth.

August 22

We owe the animals our profoundest apologies. Defenseless and unable to retaliate, they have suffered immense agonies under our domination that most of us have never witnessed or acknowledged. Now knowing better, we can act better, and acting better, we can live better, and give the animals, our children, and ourselves a true reason for hope and celebration.

August 23

We have all been born into a herding culture that commodifies animals, and we have all been affected by the cruelty, violence, and predatory competitiveness that our meals require and that our culture embodies. We've also been taught to be loyal to our culture and relatively uncritical of it, to disconnect from the monumental horror we needlessly perpetuate, and to be oblivious to the disastrous effects this has on every level of our shared and private lives.

August 24

Within us lie seeds of awakening and compassion that may be already sprouting. Our individual journeys of transformation and spiritual evolution call us to question who and what we've been told we and others are, to discover and cultivate the seeds of insight and clarity within us, and to realize the connections we've been taught to ignore.

August 25

When we uproot exclusion and domination from our plates, seeds of compassion can finally freely blossom, and this process depends primarily on us watering the seeds and fully contributing our unique journey. We depend on each other, and as we free the beings we call animals, we will regain our freedom. Loving them, we will learn to love each other and be fully loved.

August 26

Many spiritual teachers have pointed out that when we harm others, we harm ourselves even more severely. The hard-heartedness of the killer and exploiter is in itself a terrible punishment because it is a loss of sensitivity to the beauty and sacredness of life. That loss may go unrecognized, but the life itself, armored, violent, and competitive, is lived as a struggle of separateness and underlying fear, and its relations with others are poisoned.

August 27

Liberating and honoring the feminine principle is perhaps the most pressing task in our culture's evolution toward peace, sustainability, and spiritual maturity. The feminine principle, cross-culturally, is concerned fundamentally with nurturing, receptivity, making connections, intuition, and bringing forth new life.

August 28

Our prayers for peace will bear fruit when we are living the prayer for peace and, most importantly, when we offer peace to those who are at our mercy and who also long for peace and the freedom to live their lives and fulfill their purposes.

August 29

Our welfare is ultimately dependent on the welfare of others. By freeing and encouraging others we are liberated and encouraged. We can never sever our connection to all beings, but we can ignore and violate it, planting seeds of tragedy and suffering.

August 30

Honoring our natural place in the web of life by eating the foods intended for us will plant seeds of abundance, love, and freedom, whatever our religion may be.

August 31

When we look deeply enough, we discover a disturbing force that is fundamental in generating our dilemmas and crises, a force that is not actually hidden at all, but is staring up at us every day from our plates! It has been lying undiscovered all along in the most obvious of places: It is our food.

September 1

Achieving peace between human beings, from the household to the international battlefields, depends upon treating each other with respect and kindness. This will be possible when we first extend that respect and kindness to those who are at our mercy and who cannot retaliate against us.

September 2

If we are sincere in our quest for human peace, freedom, and dignity, we have no choice but to offer this to our neighbors, the animals of this Earth.

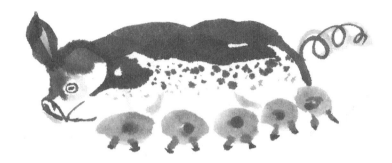

September 3

We cannot become more intimate with someone or something than by eating them. They then literally become us. Such an intimate act must certainly be attended to with the greatest awareness, love, discrimination, and reverence. If it is not, then it is a clear indication that something is seriously awry.

September 4

Joining together to pray for and visualize world peace is certainly a noble idea, but if we continue to dine on the misery of our fellow neighbors we are creating a monumental and ongoing prayer for violence, terror, and slavery. It is the prayer of our actions, and it is the experienced reality of billions of sensitive creatures who are at our mercy and to whom we show no mercy.

September 5

Until we live our prayers for peace and freedom by granting peace and freedom to those who are vulnerable in our hands, we will find neither peace nor freedom.

September 6

Joy, love, and abundance are always available to us, and will manifest in our lives to the degree that we understand that they are given to us as we give them to others. The price we must pay for love and freedom *is* the ice cream cone, the steak, and the eggnog we casually consume.

September 7

Veganism is a call for us to unite in seeing that as long as we oppress other living beings, we will inevitably create and live in a culture of oppression. Class struggle is a result of the herding culture's mentality of domination and exclusion, and is just part of the misery that is inevitably connected with eating animal foods.

September 8

As we cultivate awareness and question the death orientation that stares at us from our plates, we create a field of freedom and compassion, and as we move to plant-based meals, we can become agents of life, breathing a new spirit of protecting and including into our world that, by blessing the animals who are at our mercy, will bless us a hundredfold. This is a *radical* transformation because it goes, as the word radical implies, to the essential root of our unyielding dilemmas, the commodification of animals for food.

September 9

We universally condemn supremacism, elitism, and exclusivism for destroying peace and social justice, yet we unquestioningly and even proudly adopt precisely these attitudes when it comes to animals.

September 10

We tell ourselves that we are good, just, upright, kind and gentle people. We just happen to enjoy eating animals, which is okay because they were put here for us to use and we need the protein. Yet the extreme cruelty and violence underlying our meals is undeniable, and so our collective shadow looms larger and more menacing the more we deny its existence, sabotaging our efforts to grow spiritually and to collectively evolve a more awakened culture.

September 11

The key to reclaiming our birthright and harmony, hidden in the most obvious of places—our plates—requires (as appropriate to mythic wisdom) that for us to be free, we must first free those whom we chain. To reclaim our purpose, we must restore the purposes we have stolen from others.

September 12

The collision of soaring demand for fossil fuels with their permanently diminishing availability will cause unremitting upward price pressure as demands continue to expand and conflicts over limited oil escalate. With the coming unavoidable decline in fossil fuel availability, the days of cheap animal foods are numbered. We may begin to recognize that eating animal foods is an unacceptable waste of our limited petroleum supplies. Already people are getting outraged about the petroleum wasted by large SUVs that are inefficient compared to economy cars by a factor of perhaps three to one. Will we get similarly outraged at people eating beef, chicken, fish, eggs, and dairy products, which are inefficient compared to plant foods by factors that far exceed those of the biggest SUVs—factors of 10, 15, and 25 to one?

September 13

If we all ate a plant-based diet, we could feed ourselves on a small fraction of the land and grains that eating an animal-based diet requires. For example, researchers estimate that 2.5 acres of land can meet the food energy needs of twenty-two people eating potatoes, nineteen people eating corn, twenty-three people eating cabbage, fifteen people eating wheat, or two people eating chicken or dairy products, and only one person eating beef or eggs.

September 14

The military-industrial-meat-medical-media complex has and offers no incentive to reduce animal food consumption. Poisoning the earth with massive doses of toxic chemicals and petroleum-based fertilizers is highly profitable for the petroleum and chemical industries. These toxins cause cancer, which is highly profitable to the chemical-pharmaceutical-medical complex. While the world's rich omnivores waste precious supplies of grain, petroleum, water, and land feeding fattened animals, the world's poor have little grain to eat or clean water to drink, and their chronic hunger, thirst, and misery create conditions for war, terrorism, and drug addiction, which are extremely profitable industries as well. The richest fifth of the world's population gets obesity, heart disease, and diabetes, also highly profitable for industry.

September 15

When we eat, we are loved by the eternal and mysterious force that births all life, that makes present all who ever preceded us, that manifests itself ceaselessly as us and experiences life through us, with a love that thoroughly gives of itself to us, to we who *are* this force. It is a love that our intuitive heart can sense and respond to and deeply, ecstatically appreciate, but that our rational mind can barely begin to comprehend.

September 16

Once we realize that preparing and eating food is humanity's fundamental symbol of intimacy and spiritual transformation, we can begin to understand why sacred feasts are essential to every culture's religious and social life

September 17

Switching to a plant-based diet, we could reduce petroleum usage and imports enormously, and slash the amount of hydrocarbons and carbon dioxide that contribute to air pollution and global warming. We could save hundreds of billions of dollars per year in medical, drug, and insurance expenses, which would boost personal savings and thus reinvigorate the economy, providing fresh funds for creative projects and environmental restoration. Desolate monocropped fields devoted to livestock feed could be planted with trees, bringing back forests, streams, and wildlife. Marine ecosystems could rebuild, rain forests could begin healing, and with our demand for resources of all kinds dramatically reduced, environmental and military tension could ease.

September 18

Much of medical research today is actually an apparently desperate quest to find ways to continue eating animal foods and to escape the consequences of our cruel and unnatural practices. Do we *really* want to be successful in this?

September 19

Marx's "Workers of the world, unite!" never questioned the underlying ethic of dominating animals and nature, and hence was not truly revolutionary. It operated within the human supremacist framework and never challenged the mentality that sees living beings as commodities.

September 20

We have not begun to scratch the surface of understanding animals. How can we know what it is to swim as whales, at home in the ocean depths and migrating thousands of miles, speaking in underwater songs and breathing together in conscious harmony, or to fly in a flock of sandpipers, whirling in an effortless synchronicity, fifty birds as one, or to burrow as prairie dogs, creating complex underground communities with virtually endless chambers, passageways, and interactions?

September 21

When we look deeply we see that understanding brings and awakens love, and that love brings and awakens understanding. If our so-called understanding of animals does not ignite within us a loving urge to allow them to fulfill their lives and purposes, to honor, respect and appreciate them, then it is not true understanding. Our science is in many ways incapable of this authentic understanding, and, because it is also often a vehicle of corporate power, it is best not to rely on it too heavily in our quest for wisdom or healing.

September 22

Confronted with the problems that characterize our herding culture, we are perhaps like the metaphorical man wounded by an arrow that the Buddha discussed with his students. He said that the man would be foolish if he tried to discover who shot the arrow, why he shot it, where he was when he shot it, and so forth, before having the arrow removed and the wound treated, lest he bleed to death attempting to get his questions answered. We, likewise, can all remove the arrow and treat the wound of eating animal foods right now. We don't need to know the whole history. We can easily see it is cruel and that it is unnecessary; whatever people have done in the past, we are not obligated to imitate them if it is based on delusion.

September 23

It is the height of irony that eating a diet based on animal foods, which are complicated, wasteful, cruel, and expensive to produce, is seen as simple in our culture, and that eating a vegan diet based on plant foods, which are simple, efficient, inexpensive, and free of cruelty to produce, is seen as complicated and difficult. Nevertheless, the truth is slowly coming to light, and the pressures within the old paradigm are building as more of us refuse to see animals as objects to be eaten or used for our purposes.

September 24

Rather than relying on science to validate veganism and our basic herbivore physiology, we may do better by calling attention to universal truths: animals are undeniably capable of suffering; our physical bodies are strongly affected by thoughts, feelings, and aspirations; and we cannot reap happiness for ourselves by sowing seeds of misery for others. Nor may we be free while unnaturally enslaving others. We are all connected. These are knowings of the heart and veganism is, ultimately, a choice to listen to the wisdom in our heart as it opens to understanding the interconnectedness and essential unity of all life.

September 25
We may rationalize our meals by saying that we always thank the animal's spirit for offering her body to nourish us. If someone were to lock us up, torture us, steal our children, and then stab us to death, would we acquiesce as long as they thanked our spirit?

September 26
The vegan ideals of mercy and justice for animals have been articulated for centuries, often from within the religious establishment, and it is fascinating and instructive to see how these voices have been almost completely silenced or marginalized by the herding culture. It seems to be an unconscious reflex action. For example, if we read Jesus' teachings, we find a passionate exhortation to mercy and love, yet the possibility that the historical Jesus may have been a vegan is a radical idea for most Christians.

September 27
Jesus' message was intolerably radical, for it was the revolutionary vegan message of mercy and love for all creatures that strikes directly at the mentality of domination and exclusion that underlies both the herding culture we live in today and the culture of Jesus' time.

September 28
Voltaire wisely said, "If we believe absurdities, we will commit atrocities." Culture is the product of conversations, and our conversations are still dominated by the ideas and assumptions of the exploitive herding paradigm we were all fed as children.

September 29

All of us are celebrations of infinite mysterious Spirit, deserving of honor and respect. If our religions don't emphasize this and include all of us, it's time to replace them with spiritual teachings and traditions that do.

September 30
Our actions reinforce attitudes, in us and in others, that amplify the ripples of those actions until they become the devastating waves of insensitivity, conflict, injustice, brutality, disease, and exploitation that rock our world today.

October 1
As omnivores, we may resent vegans for reminding us of the suffering we cause, for we'd rather be comfortable and keep all the ugliness hidden, but our comfort has nothing to do with justice or with authentic inner peace. It is the comfort of blocking out and disconnecting, and it comes with a terrible price.

October 2
Religion's turning away has allowed the atrocities to continue and legitimized the turning away of the general population. This turning away is the paradigmatic learning that our culture specializes in, particularly with regard to the plight of the animals we eat and use; it is the everyday teaching of not seeing, not caring, disconnecting, and ignoring.

October 3
Taking responsibility for the violence we are causing others and ourselves through our actions, words, and thoughts is never as easy as blaming others for the violence in our world.

October 4

An interesting objection to adopting a plant-based way of eating that many Christians rely on is the saying by Jesus that "Not that which goeth into the mouth defileth a man; but that which cometh out of the mouth, this defileth a man" (Matthew 15:11). This is often interpreted as giving us permission to eat anything we like and instructing us instead to be mindful of our speech. By now it should be clear that this objection misses the point entirely. When we order a chicken or a cheeseburger at a deli, restaurant, or market, *that* is the moment that we engage in violence and cause "murders," "thefts," and suffering to defenseless animals and disadvantaged people. At that moment we are like the general who gives an order to kill someone in a faraway country; though he never sees the blood or hears the scream, he is nevertheless responsible for the killing.

October 5

Of itself, veganism is not a panacea, but it effectively removes a basic hindrance to our happiness, freedom, and unfoldment. As a living and ongoing expression of nonviolence, it is an enormously powerful agent of transformation in our individual lives, especially since our culture opposes it so vehemently.

October 6

As our culture moves toward a vegan orientation, we will see enormous healing and liberating forces unleashed. Indeed, imagining our culture as a vegan culture is truly imagining an almost completely different culture. This ever-present potential beckons to us.

October 7

Changing our individual daily food choices to reflect a consciousness of mercy will transform our lives and move our culture in a positive direction far more than any other change we can contemplate. Following right behind this change in our individual food choices is the necessity of practicing mindfulness and nonviolence in all our relations in order to bring our mind and heart into alignment with the truth of our interconnectedness, and to allow us to enter the present moment more deeply and experience directly the mystery, joy, and beauty of being.

October 8

The greatest delight is in feeling, connecting, awakening, caring, and loving, and it begins with the daily ritual that we all participate in, our most intimate connection with the created world, that we call eating.

October 9

The shadow archetype represents those aspects of ourselves that we refuse to acknowledge, the part of ourselves that we have disowned. To itself, the shadow is what the self is not, and in this case it is our own cruelty and violence that we deny and repress.

October 10

The shadow is a vital and undeniable force that cannot, in the end, be repressed. The tremendous psychological forces required to confine, mutilate, and kill millions of animals every day, and to keep the whole bloody slaughter repressed and invisible, work in two ways. One way is to numb, desensitize, and armor us, which decreases our intelligence and ability to make connections. The other is to force us to act out exactly what we are repressing. This is done through projection. We create an acceptable target to loathe for being violent, cruel, and tyrannical—the very qualities that we refuse to acknowledge in ourselves—and then we attack it.

October 11

We become spiritually and psychologically free only as we are able to see and integrate the shadow aspects of ourselves, and this will only be possible when we stop eating animal foods, relaxing and releasing the irresistible need to block our awareness. In unchaining animals, we unchain ourselves.

October 12

We will only survive and thrive if we recognize the central power of our meals to shape our consciousness. Food is eaten and becomes the physical vehicle of consciousness, and consciousness chooses what to incorporate into itself from itself. Do we cultivate and eat fear or love? Terrorized animals or nurtured plants? We cannot build a tower of love with bricks of cruelty.

October 13

Our love, to actually *be* love, must be acted upon and lived. Developing our capacity for love is not only the means of evolution; it is the end as well, and when we fully embody love, we will know the truth of our oneness with all life. This makes us free

October 14

Evolution implies not only change but transformation. In world mythology, when heroes refuse the call to leave home to take the evolutionary journey, they become sick. For us as a culture it is the same.

October 15

The lesson is quite basic. If we can't stop the cruelty of eating animal foods, how can we presume to develop the sensitivity, the spiritual consciousness, the joy, peace, and creative freedom that are our potential?

October 16

Intuition liberates, connects, illumines—and threatens our herding culture's underlying paradigm of violent oppression of animals and of the feminine. Intuition sees the shadow clearly, and disarms it by embracing it and not feeding it. It sees the animal hidden in the hot dog, ice cream, and omelette, feels her misery and fear, and embraces her with love.

October 17

We are not predatory by nature, but we've been taught that we are, in the most potent way possible: we've been raised from birth to eat like predators. We've thus been initiated into a predatory culture and been forced to see ourselves at the deepest levels as predators.

October 18

Authentic spiritual teachings must necessarily teach an ethics of loving-kindness, because this reflects our interconnectedness and the truth that what we give out comes back to us. It leads to the harmony in relationships that is necessary not just for social progress, but also for our individual inner peace and spiritual progress.

October 19

We can see that in general, the more a culture oppresses animals, the greater its inner agitation and numbness, and the more extroverted and dominating it tends to be. This is related to the scarcity of meditation in Western cultures, where people are uncomfortable with sitting still. Quiet, open contemplation would allow the repressed guilt and violence of the animal cruelty in meals to emerge to be healed and released. Instead, the very activities that would be most beneficial to people of our herding culture are the activities that are the most studiously avoided.

October 20

Shojin is "religious abstention from animal foods" and is based on the core religious teaching of *ahimsa*, or harmlessness, the practice of refraining from causing harm to other sentient beings. Shojin and samadhi are seen to work together, with shojin purifying the body-mind and allowing, though certainly not guaranteeing, access to the spiritually enriching experience of samadhi. Outer compassion and inner stillness feed each other. Shojin and veganism are essential to our spiritual health because they remove a fundamental hindrance on our path.

October 21

The motivation behind vegan living is the universal spiritual principle of compassion that has been articulated both secularly and through the world's religious traditions; the difference lies in veganism's insistence that this compassion be actually practiced. The words of Donald Watson, who created the term "vegan" in 1944, reveal this practical orientation and bear repeating:

"Veganism denotes a philosophy and way of living which seeks to exclude, as far as is possible and practicable, all forms of exploitation of, and cruelty to, animals for food, clothing, or any other purpose; and by extension promotes the development and use of animal-free alternatives for the benefit of humans, animals, and the environment."

October 22

All the world's major religions have their own form of the Golden Rule that teaches kindness to others as the essence of their message. They all recognize animals as sentient and vulnerable to us, and include them within the moral sphere of our behavior.

October 23

Buckminster Fuller often emphasized that the way of cultural transformation is not so much in fighting against destructive attitudes and practices, but in recognizing them as being obsolete and offering positive, higher-level alternatives. The competitive, violent, commodifying mentality of the ancient herding cultures is, in our age of nuclear weapons and global interconnectedness, profoundly obsolete, as is eating the animal foods of these old cultures, which are unhealthy in the extreme both to our body-minds and to our precious planetary ecology.

October 24

We can argue that animals are largely unconscious, decreeing that because animals seem to lack the complex language that allows them to formulate thoughts in words as we do, their experience of suffering must therefore be less significant or intense for them. This same thinking, however, could be used to justify harming human infants and senile elderly people. If anything, beings who lack the ability to analyze their circumstances may suffer at our hands more intensely than we would because they are unable to put the distance of internal dialogue between themselves and their suffering.

October 25

Because of our herding orientation and our unassuaged guilt complex due to the misery in our daily meals, we have warped our sacred connection with the infinite loving source of our life to an ultimate irony: comparing ourselves to sheep, we beg our shepherd for mercy, but since we show no mercy, we fear deep down we'll not be shown mercy either and live in dread of our inevitable death. We bargain and may proclaim overconfidently that we're saved and our sins are forgiven (no matter what atrocities we mete out to animals and people outside our in-group), or we may reject the whole conventional religious dogma as so much absurd pablum and rely on the shallow materialism of science. However it happens, our spiritual impulse is inevitably repressed and distorted by the fear, guilt, violence, hardness, competitiveness, and shallow reductionism that herding and eating animals always demands.

October 26

Recognizing the insanity of our actions and beliefs is the first and essential step to healing and awakening.

October 27

By living the truth of compassion in our meals and daily lives, we can create a field of peace, love, and freedom that can radiate into our world and bless others by silently and subtly encouraging the same in them.

October 28

Who are we? What is our proper role on this earth? I submit we can only begin to discover these answers if we first take the vegan imperative seriously and live compassionately toward other creatures. Then peace with each other will at least be possible, as well as a deeper understanding of the mysteries of healing, freedom, and love.

October 29

By ceasing to eat animal foods and thus causing misery to our neighbors, and by practicing meditation and quiet reflection, which can eventually extract our consciousness out of the brambles of compulsive thinking, we can begin to understand what consciousness actually is. We will see that to the degree we can be open to the present moment and dwell in inner spacious silence, beyond the ceaseless internal dialogue of the busy mind, we can experience the radiant, joy-filled serenity of pure consciousness.

October 30

So what are we, and what are animals? Our concepts only reveal our impeding conditioning. We are neighbors, mysteries, and we are all manifestations of the eternal light of the infinite consciousness that has birthed and maintains what we call the universe. The intuitive knowing that would reveal this to us, though, is mostly unavailable because as a culture we are outer-directed and fail to cultivate the inner resources and discipline that would allow us to access this deeper wisdom.

October 31

It is vital that we all contribute to the positive revolution for which our future is calling.

November 1

The American roots of deeply questioning food and developing the philosophical foundation for a more compassionate relationship with animals can be traced to the progressive writers clustered around Emerson in Concord in the mid-nineteenth century. Thoreau wrote, "I have no doubt that it is a part of the destiny of the human race in its gradual improvement, to leave off eating animals as surely as the savage tribes have left off eating each other when they came into contact with the more civilized."

November 2

The desensitizing of millions of children and adults—on the massive scale that consuming millions of tortured animals daily requires—sows countless seeds of human violence, war, poverty, and despair. These outcomes are unavoidable, for we can never reap joy, peace, and freedom for ourselves while sowing the seeds of harming and enslaving others.

November 3

Within us lie seeds of awakening and compassion that may be already sprouting. Our individual journeys of transformation and spiritual evolution call us to question who and what we've been told we and others are, to discover and cultivate the seeds of insight and clarity within us, and to realize the connections we've been taught to ignore. As we do this and as our web of journeys interweaves within our culture, cross-fertilizing and planting seeds, we can continue the transformation that is now well underway, and transcend the obsolete old paradigm that generates cycles of violence.

November 4

When we uproot exclusion and domination from our plates, seeds of compassion can finally freely blossom, and this process depends primarily on us watering the seeds and fully contributing our unique journey. We depend on each other, and as we free the beings we call animals, we will regain our freedom. Loving them, we will learn to love each other and be fully loved.

November 5

The more forcefully we ignore something, the more power it has over us and the more strongly it influences us.

November 6

Emerson's "You have just dined, and however scrupulously the slaughter-house is concealed in the graceful distance of miles, there is complicity," shows the esteemed Concord sage's ability to make the connections that elude most. Bronson Alcott's daughter, Louisa May, wrote, "Vegetable diet and sweet repose. Animal food and nightmare. Pluck your body from the orchard; do not snatch it from the shambles. Without flesh diet there could be no bloodshedding war." She makes explicit the connection between the violence inherent in eating animals, nightmares, and the nightmare of human violence turned against ourselves.

November 7

Our earth will naturally heal when we stop killing fish and sea life and polluting and wasting water in such unsustainable ways. Forests and wildlife will return because we'll need far less farmland to feed everyone a plant-based diet, and the whole earth will be relieved of the unbearable pressure exerted by omnivorous humans. We will be released from the paralysis that prevents us from creatively addressing the looming depletion of fossil fuels and the other challenges we face.

November 8

None of us ever consciously and freely chose to eat animals. We have all inherited this from our culture and upbringing. Going into the baby food department of any grocery store today, we see it immediately: beef-flavored baby food, chicken, veal, and lamb baby food, and even cheese lasagna baby food. Well-meaning parents, grandparents, friends, and neighbors have forced the flesh and secretions of animals upon us from before we can remember.

November 9

Compassion is ethical intelligence: it is the capacity to make connections and the consequent urge to act to relieve the suffering of others.

November 10

Making the effort to cultivate our awareness and see beyond the powerful acculturation we endured brings understanding. Healing, grace and freedom come from understanding. Love understands. From understanding, we can embrace our responsibility and become a force for blessing the world with our lives, rather than perpetuating disconnectedness and cruelty by proxy.

November 11

As our web of journeys interweaves within our culture, cross-fertilizing and planting seeds, we can continue the transformation that is now well underway, and transcend the obsolete old paradigm that generates cycles of violence.

November 12

Two types of agriculture emerged—plant and animal—and the distinction between them is significant. Growing plants and gardening is more feminine work; plants are tended and nurtured, and as we work with the cycles of nature, we are part of a process that enhances and amplifies life. It is life-affirming and humble (from *humus*, earth) work that supports our place in the web of life. On the other hand, large animal agriculture or husbandry was always men's work and required violent force from the beginning, to contain powerful animals, control them, guard them, castrate them and, in the end, kill them.

November 13

When we cultivate mindful awareness of the consequences of our food choices and conscientiously adopt a plant-based way of eating, refusing to participate in the domination of animals and the dulling of awareness this requires, we make a profound statement that both flows from and reinforces our ability to make connections. We become a force of sensitivity, healing, and compassion.

November 14

Cultivating awareness, we can transcend the imposed view that animals are mere food objects. With this, we will see consumerism, pornography, and the disconnectedness that leads inexorably to slavery and self-destruction evaporate.

November 15

The contemporary vegan movement is founded on loving-kindness and mindfulness of our effects on others. It is revolutionary because it transcends and renounces the violent core of the herding culture in which we live. It is founded on living the truth of interconnectedness and thereby consciously minimizing the suffering we impose on animals, humans, and biosystems; it frees us *all* from the slavery of becoming mere commodities. It signifies the birth of a new consciousness, the resurrection of intelligence and compassion, and the basic rejection of cruelty and domination. It is our only real hope for the future of our species because it addresses the cause rather than being concerned merely with effects.

November 16

It's funny how we want transformation without having to change! Yet the fundamental transformation called for today requires the most fundamental change—a change in our relationship to food and to animals, which will cause a change in our behavior.

November 17

Farming animals is simply a refined and perverse form of predation in which the animals are confined before being attacked and killed. It doesn't stop with animals, however.

November 18

In our churches, ministers often speak about the tragedy of loving things and using people, when we must instead love people and use things. After the services, people eat meals in which animals have become things to be used, not loved. This action, ritually repeated, propels us into using people just as we use animals—as things.

November 19

Instead of reducing our intelligence and compassion by denying and destroying the intelligence and purpose of animals, we could celebrate, honor, and appreciate the immense diversity of intelligences, beauties, abilities, and gifts that animals possess and contribute to our world. We could liberate ourselves by liberating them and allowing them to fulfill the purposes that their particular intelligences yearn for. We could respect their lives and treat them with kindness. Our awareness and compassion would flourish, bringing more love and wisdom into our relationships with each other.

November 20

Most of us resist being told we've been indoctrinated. After all, we live in the land of the free, and we like to think we've arrived freely at the belief that we need to eat animal products and that it's natural and right to do so. In fact, we have inherited this belief. We've been indoctrinated in the most deeply rooted and potent way possible, as vulnerable infants, yet because our culture denies the existence of indoctrination, the reality of the process is invisible, making it difficult for most of us to realize or admit the truth.

November 21

We have become a culture that craves noise, distraction, busyness, and entertainment at all costs. This allows our eaten violence to remain buried, blocked, denied, and righteously projected.

November 22

In questioning our culture's most fundamental and defining practice, that of imprisoning and brutalizing animals for food, we practice leaving home and embark on a spiritual journey that will put us fundamentally at odds with our culture's values, but that at the same time makes it possible for us to be heroes who can help uplift and transform our ailing culture.

November 23

By questioning our inherited cultural conditioning to commodify, abuse, and eat animals, we are taking the greatest step we can to leave home, become responsible adults, and mature spiritually, and by actively helping others do the same, we return home with a liberating message of compassion and truth that can inspire and bless others. By leaving home we can find our true home, contribute to social progress, and help the animals with whom we share this precious earth have a chance to be at home again as well.

November 24

There are strong voices in all religious traditions emphasizing that our kindness to other beings should be based on compassion. This is more than merely being open to the suffering of others; it also explicitly includes the urge to *act* to relieve their suffering. We are thus responsible not just to refrain from harming animals and humans, but also to do what we can to stop others from harming them, and to create conditions that educate, inspire, and help others to live in ways that show kindness and respect for all life. This is the high purpose to which the core teachings of the world's wisdom traditions call us. It is an evolutionary imperative, a spiritual imperative, an imperative of compassion, and, in reality, a vegan imperative.

November 25

A basic reason that billions of animals suffer confinement and slaughter is our cultural belief that we need to eat animal-derived foods to be healthy, yet one of the most common motivations many of us have to reduce or eliminate animal food consumption is improving our health! Illuminating this paradox requires us to investigate our human physiology and the animal foods we eat, and to reconnect with the perennial understanding that cultivating kindness and awareness improves physical and mental health, while harmfulness and unconsciousness lead ultimately to physical and mental disease.

November 26

We could live in far greater harmony with the universal intelligence that is the source of our life. To do so, however, we would have to stop viewing animals as commodities, and this means we would have to stop viewing them as food.

November 27

Like all animals, we are essentially spiritual beings, manifestations of a universal, loving intelligence that has given us bodies designed to thrive on the abundant foods that we can peacefully nourish and gather in orchards, fields, and gardens.

November 28

Geniuses like Pythagoras, Leonardo da Vinci, and Mahatma Gandhi abstained from eating animals. Plutarch wrote, "When we clog and cloy our body with flesh, we also render our mind and intellect coarse. When the body's clogged with unnatural food, the mind becomes confused and dull and loses its cheerfulness. Such minds engage in trivial pursuits, because they lack the clearness and vigor for higher thinking."

November 29

The animal food culture promotes domination and exploitation of the female and the feminine, which are full of life-giving and nurturing powers, and of infants and children, who are full of the powers of innocence and growth.

November 30

It's ironic that the burden of justifying possible nutritional deficiencies rests on vegans ("where do you get your protein/vitamin B-12/etc.?"), because research shows that vegans typically have twice the fruit and vegetable intake of people eating the standard American diet. In recent studies, vegans had higher intakes of sixteen out of the nineteen nutrients studied, including three times more vitamin C, vitamin E, and fiber, twice the folate, magnesium, copper, and manganese, and more calcium and plenty of protein. Vegans also had half the saturated fat intake, one-sixth the rate of being overweight, and, while vegans were shown to be at risk for deficiencies in three nutrients (calcium, iodine, and vitamin B-12), people eating the standard American diet were at risk for deficiencies in seven nutrients (calcium, iodine, vitamin C, vitamin E, fiber, folate, and magnesium).

December 1

Buying organically grown produce, grains, beans, and nuts is important not just because they're higher in vitamins and minerals, but also because the toxic runoff from conventional agriculture poisons streams and people, and kills birds, fish, insects, and wildlife. The amount of toxins used to produce a head of lettuce or bowl of rice is still, however, far less than that used to produce a hot dog, cheese omelet, or piece of catfish because animal foods require enormous quantities of pesticide-laden feed grain to produce.

December 2

The suffering that food animals undergo, the suffering of those who eat them and profit by them, the suffering of starving people who could be fed with the grain that feeds these animals, and the suffering we thoughtlessly impose on the ecosystem, other creatures, and future generations are all interconnected. It is this interconnectedness of suffering, and its reverse, of love, caring, and awareness, that calls out for our understanding.

December 3

Achieving this transformation means living the truth of love and authentically comprehending our interconnectedness, and not merely talking about it. It means changing our thinking and our behavior—how we view animals and what we eat. As we recognize our shadow and become free of it, compassion returns and we naturally stop feeding it with our diet of hidden terror.

December 4

All four of the possible paths that a calf born on a dairy may take are paths of abuse and early death. Since cows in the wild easily live twenty to thirty years, the industry, in killing calves, steers, and dairy cows at the ages of several months to several years, is really killing infants and children. In this it is the same as the industries that confine and kill lambs, pigs, chickens, turkeys, and fish: all are pushed to grow abnormally quickly and are slaughtered young. Similarly, in the wars we inflict upon each other, children suffer and die the most, and more than ever they are even forced to do the killing.

December 5

The protein in milk, particularly casein, while perfect for baby cows, is too large and difficult for us to digest. Calves have a particular enzyme, rennin, not present in humans, that coagulates and helps breaks down casein. According to renowned nutrition researcher T. Colin Campbell, "Cows' milk protein may be the single most significant chemical carcinogen to which humans are exposed."

December 6

It is exciting to contemplate educational, economic, governmental, religious, medical, and other institutions based on honoring and protecting the rights and interests of both animals and humans. When as a culture we stop commodifying creatures, a new world of kindness, fairness, cooperation, peace, and freedom will naturally unfold in human relations as well.

December 7

Enslaving and eating animals is relentlessly polluting our mental and bodily environments, hardening our hearts and blocking feelings and awareness, instigating fear, violence, and repression in our relationships, laying waste our precious planet, gruesomely torturing and killing billions of terrorized beings, deadening us spiritually, and profoundly disempowering us by impeding our innate intelligence and our ability to make essential connections.

December 8

There is no way to overstate the magnitude of the collective spiritual transformation that will occur when we shift from food of violent oppression to food of gentleness and compassion.

December 9

The key to veganism is that it is lived. No one can be a vegetarian in theory only! Unlike many religious teachings that are primarily theoretical and internal, veganism is solidly practical. The motivation of veganism is compassion. It is not at all about personal purity or individual health or salvation, except as these bless others. It is a concrete, visible way of living that flows from, and reinforces, a sense of caring and connectedness.

December 10

As we make connections and become open to feedback, it will be increasingly obvious that one of the greatest gifts any of us can give to the world, to the human family, to future generations, to animals, to ourselves, and to our loved ones is to go vegan and dedicate our lives to encouraging others to do the same.

December 11

Being willing to look, see, respond, and reconnect with all our neighbors and live this interconnectedness inspires us naturally to choose food, entertainment, clothing, and products that cause a minimum of unnecessary cruelty to vulnerable living beings. As we do this, we become more mindful of the ripples our actions cause in the world. Our spiritual transformation deepens, and as our sensitivity increases we yearn to bless others more and to be a voice for the voiceless.

December 12

The more we connect, the more we understand and the more we love, and this love propels us not only to leave home, questioning our culture's attitude of domination and exclusion, but also to return home, speaking on behalf of those who are vulnerable.

December 13

The spiritual revolution needs all of us, whatever our religious beliefs, ethnicity, class, or other variables may be. Every one of us has a piece of the puzzle to contribute, and our overall success depends on each of us discovering our talents and passion and persistently contributing them.

December 14

We are only comfortable eating animals when we exclude them from the categories we use to define ourselves, but our differences from animals are far less than our eating habits force us to believe they are.

December 15

The more we live in alignment with our values, the stronger the truth-field we emanate will be, and the more our words, gestures, and actions will carry weight with perpetrators.

December 16

The new extremes to which animals are now subjected without remorse or awareness require that we adopt a more radically conscientious orientation that addresses the roots of our violent mentality. While it may seem extreme to our mainstream culture to advocate for a vegan revolution that utterly rejects our commodification of animals, it is only such an apparently extreme position that can be an antidote to the extreme abuse we now force upon animals.

December 17

In fact, veganism is not extreme from the point of view of our innate nature, which longs for love, creativity, and spiritual evolution.

December 18

It is problematic to determine whether our lives as humans have actually improved over the centuries and millennia, for all our valiant efforts. Although we have comforts and possibilities undreamt of by our forebears, we also have stresses, diseases, and frustrations that they could not possibly have imagined. For animals, however, the situation has plainly deteriorated, especially over the more recent human generations.

December 19

None of us is completely innocent, because to some degree we all are, and have been, in all three roles as victims, perpetrators, and bystanders.

December 20

People who are serious about spiritual growth are apparently capable of embracing fundamental change in their lives, and may even welcome the opportunity.

December 21

We exhibit not only hubris but remarkable obtuseness in caging, torturing, and infecting animals in the name of improving our health. We can see the outcome of our actions already, as new diseases continue to arise and old ones spread, often becoming impervious to our increasingly devastating drugs.

December 22

As we research, discuss, and deepen our understanding of the mind-body connection, of the human-animal connection, and of our connection with all the larger wholes in which we are embedded, our spiritual purpose will become manifest.

December 23

Because the quality of our food is directly connected to our mental and physiological health and to our quality of life, diminishing the quality of our food can make us sicker, weaker, and more distracted, violent, stressed, drugged, confused, and disempowered. This is perhaps the real agenda behind the vicious efforts to weaken the standards for organic foods and to introduce highly toxic foods through irradiation, genetic engineering, addition of artificial dyes, noxious flavor-enhancers like MSG, chemical preservatives, known carcinogens like NutraSweet, and dangerous genetically engineered hormones like rBGH and carcinogenic growth hormones. This is in addition to promoting animal-based meals, which concentrate the largest variety and intensity of toxins and are inherently confusing and disempowering.

December 24

We are all presented with the same evidence and hear the same call for mercy and justice.

December 25

Jesus' exhortation that we love one another and not do to others what we wouldn't want done to us is the essence of the vegan ethic, which is a boundless compassion that includes all who can suffer by our actions.

December 26

Rising above anger and despair while still keeping our hearts open to the ocean of cruelty, indifference, and suffering on this earth is not easy. It requires cultivating wisdom and compassion—both the inner silent receptivity that links us to the eternal truth of our being and the outer actions of serving and helping others that give meaning to our life.

December 27

Glimpsing this essential nature that we share with all beings not only deepens our yearning to relieve their suffering but also strengthens our ability to work effectively to do so. Seeing victims and perpetrators not merely in these roles but in their spiritual perfection and completeness is profoundly healing. We see that there are no enemies—no essentially evil people or completely hopeless or destructive situations. There are, rather, opportunities to grow, learn, serve, and work together to raise consciousness and bring compassion and understanding to the painful and unjust situations we may see unfolding around us.

December 28

As we bless others, we are blessed, and seeing beings rather than things, our own being is liberated and enriched.

December 29

The metaphor of eating is central to spiritual communion with the divine presence. It is universally recognized that eating food is both a literally and symbolically sacred action: it is directly partaking of the infinite order that transcends our finite lives.

December 30

The transnational corporations profit from animal food consumption, as do the big banks, which have made the loans that have built the whole complex and demand a healthy return on their investments. The system spreads relentlessly and globally, and while corporate and bank returns may be healthy, people, animals, and ecosystems throughout the world fall ill and are exploited and destroyed.

December 31

Everyone on this Earth could be fed easily because we currently grow more than enough grain to feed ten billion people; our current practice of feeding this grain to untold billions of animals and eating them forces over a billion of us to endure chronic malnutrition and starvation while another billion suffer from the obesity, diabetes, heart disease, and cancer linked with eating diets high in animal foods.

Conclusion

The message at the heart of *The World Peace Diet* is encouraging and inspirational. We can give thanks daily that we can feed everyone on this abundant Earth much healthier and more compassionate food on a fraction of the land, water, and other resources that we are currently using. We are all gifted with bodies that don't require any animal to suffer to obtain all the nutrients needed to celebrate our lives on this beautiful planet. Every day, we can help heal our outer world, and our inner world as well, by questioning the devastating culturally-mandated story that animals are mere commodities to be used for food and other products.

By co-creating new narratives founded upon science-based truths underlying nutritional, environmental, and social health, and our inner wisdom regarding our emotional and spiritual health, we can transform the forces destroying the interconnected web of life here. We are, it seems, in the midst of an urgent birthing process, and every effort we make as individuals to co-create and support a new narrative that liberates animals helps also to liberate humanity from violence, injustice, and disease.

May each of us awaken to our true nature and participate in the ongoing transformation of human consciousness, so that we are living our lives on this abundant Earth as we are intended, fulfilling our purpose here with creativity and appreciation for the boundless gifts that are all around us, within us, and within all our relations.

Thank you for hearing the call during these critical times, and for your efforts to participate in this birthing process. Every day is another opportunity to contribute to the awakening of humanity. May these jewels from *The World Peace Diet* serve as inspirations and reminders from your inner wisdom that radiate into your daily thoughts and actions, bringing joy, freedom, and abundance to you and to our world.

Sources of Excerpts

The page numbers below are for all editions of *The World Peace Diet*.

Titles of articles are listed at the end of this section.

(All articles are at WorldPeaceDiet.com under Will's Essays, Pre-2014)

Biographical Notes

Dr. Will Tuttle is author of the best-selling *The World Peace Diet*, published in 16 languages. A recipient of the Courage of Conscience Award and the Empty Cages Prize, he is also the author of *Your Inner Islands: The Keys to Intuitive Living,* as well as editor of *Circles of Compassion* and *Buddhism and Veganism.* A vegan since 1980 and former Zen monk in the Korean Zen tradition, he is featured in a number of documentary films. The creator of several wellness and advocacy programs, he is a frequent radio, television, and online presenter, and lectures extensively worldwide.

Madeleine Tuttle is a visionary artist from Switzerland who specializes in painting that celebrates the beauty of animals and nature. She is also a flautist, Waldorf school teacher, long-time vegan cook and coach, gardener, clothing designer, multi-media artisan, and devoted meditator. Her extensive travels on six continents and formal training in Japan in ink brush painting lend a Zen style to her work.

James Aspey is an Australian vegan activist who took a one-year vow of silence to raise awareness for animal rights and wellness. His story went viral in 2015, and he's well known for his inspirational speeches and vegan lifestyle videos, one of which has over six million views.

For information about *The World Peace Diet* and the writings, music, art, videos, trainings, and current schedule of events of Dr. Will & Madeleine Tuttle, please see WorldPeaceDiet.com.

For information regarding the World Peace Diet Online Facilitator Training Program, please see WorldPeaceMastery.com.

51269087R00087

Made in the USA
Columbia, SC
18 February 2019